101

WAYS TO MOTIVATE ATHLETES

Keith Manos

ISBN: 1-58518-961-8
Library of Congress Control Number: 2005938995
Book layout: Deborah Oldenburg
Cover design: Jeanne Hamilton
Front cover photo: Jamie Squire/Getty Images

Coaches Choice
P.O. Box 1828
Monterey, CA 93942
www.coacheschoice.com

Dedication

For my family—my parents, sisters, brother, wife, and children.
They have motivated me all my life.

Contents

Introduction

All coaches love the self-motivated athlete. Unfortunately, relatively few athletes have the self-motivation to give maximum effort when they have the belief that only minimum effort is needed. A common lament of many coaches is that their athletes are, in fact, unmotivated, that they don't work hard enough, that they're not willing to sacrifice to achieve success. "Why aren't they motivated?" they complain. "Don't they want to win?" Furthermore, too many coaches expect that the athletes who arrive for that first practice are already motivated because they have decided to give up time after school to participate.

Clearly, it is a common mistake to take motivation for granted. Coaches need to understand what motivates athletes to participate in any sport, how athletes stay motivated, and how motivation influences athletic performance. This book offers coaches of all sports proven methods for getting and keeping athletes motivated.

1

The Pre-Season

Ronald Martinez/Getty Images

#1: Be Motivated Yourself

As the coach, you will probably be the most motivated individual on the team and, therefore, should consistently exhibit the traits of a motivated person. How you act and what you say—especially what you say—should always reflect motivational signals to your athletes. In fact, tell your athletes what motivates you, then be a model of motivation at all times.

The act of motivating is in its simplest terms a means of fostering a strong belief in you and your program. You establish this belief through the sincerity of what you say and the intensity of how you say it. You can motivate some athletes simply by creating a positive image of yourself—strong, smart, decisive—and you have to work at that image, like a public relations firm does for a client corporation. In addition, when athletes see you working on the quality of your image, it will encourage them to do the following:

- Maximize their efforts in practice and games
- Be enthusiastic about their place on the squad
- Maintain persistence toward a specified goal
- Handle obstacles, failures, and criticism without quitting the team
- Be intense during competition
- Improve their physical and mental skills
- Display a positive attitude
- Be attentive and alert during practices and contests
- Express an enjoyment for practicing and competing
- Work cooperatively with teammates and coaches

The coach is truly a salesman, selling a love for the sport, dialoging about its benefits, inviting athletes to participate, and offering them rewards for that participation. You must always be meeting and challenging the personal needs each athlete brings to the sport. Indeed, coaching is motivating, and motivating kids takes work. That is why you have to be motivated. Your athletes must see that above all else.

#2: Remain Positive

James "Doc" Counsilman, a former United States Olympic swim coach and head coach at Indiana University, regularly motivated his swimmers by maintaining a positive attitude around them. He made sure they recognized the progress they were making toward their goals and worked hard to build their self-esteem. His swimmers, in turn, felt secure in their positions on the team and welcomed all challenges.

This approach should be duplicated with all athletes. If you keep reminding your athletes of their goals and their accomplishments, they will be more likely to handle any obstacle, failure, or criticism they confront during the season. When they know that they will always hear positive feedback from you, they will be more loyal to you and more likely to recognize their potential for success in competitions. Positivity is especially important following setbacks. Teach your athletes to see these setbacks as stepping stones, not stumbling blocks, to future success.

By maintaining an optimistic outlook about the season, the team, and the individuals, you can make your athletes' memories of you as their coach positive as well. Competing under you will have been a satisfying experience, something they can then share with the athletes that follow them.

When you detect athletes with poor self-images, help them remove any negative beliefs. Remind them daily that they are competent, successful athletes to force that message into their minds. And tell your kids in practice how they're getting better, that their training has made them stronger, quicker, and more skilled. This entire process may take time, maybe an entire season, but it is time well spent.

#3: Research Your Athletes

Coaches must understand that coaching today is more than a practice plan attached to a clipboard, statistics punched into a computer, or a championship plaque placed in a trophy case at the end of the season. To succeed today, you have to put more effort into researching your own athletes than scouting your opponents. Each season brings new athletes with different backgrounds, experiences, and motivations, even if they are returning letter winners. To motivate them it is imperative first to research each one individually and, second, to use that information to guide them through an often difficult and challenging season. Discover and exploit each athlete's level of aspiration: What are their goals? What are they shooting for? What are their expectations?

"I think to be effective you have to really know your athletes and be able to adapt to the situation to fit the needs of each one," says one Ohio college coach. "Everyone is a little different, and I like seeing how far they can progress."

The first and most obvious step is to have brief, informal discussions during which you ask each athlete about his interests and background. This is, of course, a more personal and time-consuming way of discovering information, but it often leads to a closer relationship between you and each athlete, which is important if you are going to spend a lot of time together. Ask the following questions: Why do you like our sport? Does competition excite you? What do you like about practices? What don't you like?

These conversations can take place before homeroom, during study halls, or after school in the preseason. Lunch time is another possibility if the athlete doesn't mind giving up time with friends.

Another way to learn more about your athletes is to have them complete a brief questionnaire in their homerooms (Figure 3-1). This survey identifies an athlete's perceptions of athletic achievement. Do they consider talent more important than attitude, strength more essential than hard work? The results provide insights into the athlete's view of his own potential to succeed.

You can obtain a more comprehensive psychological profile of each athlete with a competitive behavior questionnaire (Figure 3-2). The results will enable you to discern in detail an athlete's mental approach to competition and any anxieties he may have. Scores in the 46 to 56 range suggest a high level of tension, 36 to 45 is moderate or average, and athletes who total 35 points or less typically suffer little anxiety about competition.

The next research should focus on your athletes' sources of motivation. A survey of junior high and senior high athletes indicates the primary reason most kids participate in any sport is for affiliation; that is, they like socializing with others. For others, the key

Name _____

What does it take to be a successful athlete?

Please rate the following items from 1–15 in regards to being a successful athlete—with 1 being the most important item and 15 being the least important:

_____ Dedication and determination

_____ Strength

_____ Ability to concentrate

_____ Flexibility

_____ Good positive mental attitude

_____ Talent

_____ Intelligence

_____ Confidence

_____ Competitive drive

_____ Quickness and mobility

_____ Good physical conditioning

_____ Liking the sport (enthusiasm)

_____ Ability to cooperate with others

_____ Coordination and agility

_____ Self-motivation

Figure 3-1. Successful athlete questionnaire

Name _____ Date _____

How Competitive Are You?

Circle the number under the choice that best describes you, being sure to respond truthfully to each statement.

Statement	Always	Sometimes	Never
1. I get nervous when people watch me compete.	3	2	1
2. I have trouble sleeping before a contest.	3	2	1
3. I can't focus after making a mistake.	3	2	1
4. I perform better in practice than a match.	3	2	1
5. I make more mistakes when the score is close.	3	2	1
6. I get angry at myself when I make mistakes in a competition.	3	2	1
7. When a coach yells I lose my focus.	3	2	1
8. I get easily distracted before a contest.	3	2	1
9. The more challenging the competition, the worse I perform.	3	2	1
10. I don't like to think about the contest because it makes me too nervous.	3	2	1
11. I worry a lot about getting injured.	3	2	1
12. I usually feel sick or weak before a contest.	3	2	1
13. I rarely listen to my coach during a contest.	3	2	1
14. I'm usually disappointed by the outcomes of my competitions.	3	2	1
15. I constantly think about my performance.	3	2	1
16. The butterflies bother me throughout a competition.	3	2	1
17. The bigger the crowd, the more worried or tense I become.	3	2	1
18. I have trouble focusing after an official makes a bad call against me.	3	2	1

Total Score _____

Figure 3-2. Competitive behavior questionnaire

motivation could be an intrinsic need to perform successfully or an extrinsic need to gain rewards. A minority simply enjoy pressure and competition. Use Figure 3-3 to learn more about each athlete's personal motivation.

How do athletes stay motivated once the season begins? As long as they are enjoying the sport (and competitions), sustaining friendships, and achieving some success, they will continue competing, according to the study of 8000 athletes ages 10 to 18 by Martha Ewing and Vern Seefleldt, professors at Michigan State University. Their study also suggests that athletes will quit if they have accomplished their goal(s), have poor relations with teammates, or experience communication problems with the coach.

If motivation is a psychological stimulus that can prompt athletes to perform their best in competitions, then you must begin by studying your athletes' mental approach to competing.

- What are their personal interests?
- Why have they chosen to become members of the team?
- How committed are they to the program?
- What has motivated them in the past?
- What motivational strategies have failed on them in the past?
- How have they handled adversity in the past?

Once you accept this responsibility to research your athletes, you are more likely to build strong relationships with them and, in turn, enjoy a loyal following. Plus, you should see a growth in both the self-esteem and physical skills of athletes who will appreciate that you see them as individuals and understand their personalities.

Survey Questions

Name _____ Grade _____

Homeroom _____

Address _____

Phone _____ Birth date _____

1. What has been your greatest commitment to date?

2. What will make this sport fun for you?

3. What could be a great achievement for you this year?

4. What are your personal goals this year?

5. What are you willing to do to accomplish your goals?

6. What motivates you?

Figure 3-3. Motivation survey

#4: Have a Preseason Team Meeting

A survey of nearly 3,100 high schools across the country revealed that 82% of those schools' athletic groups held preseason team meetings. The tone and tempo of the season are revealed in these meetings, and a positive first impression is crucial. You have to be prepared for this very important meeting because it can have a major effect on your players' motivation.

Therefore, be organized and enthusiastic at this first meeting. You must begin on time and quickly establish your credibility. The athletes should learn your background, expectations, and personality through a brief, but detailed, introduction. What the athletes learn about you is important, but you also need to learn some things about them. Have them complete a personal data form.

Distribute on paper or display on a chalk board the agenda of the meeting, and be sure that all distractions are eliminated. Introduce assistant coaches and any related personnel (trainers, managers) and clarify their responsibilities and authority.

A discussion about the team's goals and direction should cover effort and eligibility, commitment and courage, rules and respect, sacrifice and success. Invite them to contribute ideas about team goals and practices. What are their expectations? What activities have helped them win in the past? What kind of thing hasn't worked?

Establish that you are in partnership with them and that your primary goal is to empower them to compete successfully. Explain that you are committed to coaching them and that you expect them to be "coachable". Be sure to conclude on a positive note and remind them of the date, time, and place of their first practice. This opening meeting has to be as much about inspiration as it does information.

#5: Order Cool Clothes

All athletes love new equipment and stylish uniforms. Therefore, if funds are available, either through your athletic department or booster club, order some cool clothes. Invite returning letter winners to submit suggestions or even select the uniforms or warm-up gear they would like to wear the following season. This can be tremendously motivating.

You could also order team hats, T-shirts, or sweaters. Consider jerseys, warm-up tops, or sweatshirts that have their names (or nicknames) on the back. Even new socks, jocks, and bandannas are appreciated by athletes.

New uniforms and other apparel can attract attention, enhance performance, and encourage motivation. Moreover, try to purchase uniforms for every level, not just the varsity. Hand-me-downs are hand-me-downs, regardless of their age, and younger athletes deserve new equipment as much as the older ones. Your players will appreciate this and probably perform with greater intensity and motivation in competitions.

#6: Polish Up Your Facilities

The intent here is to keep facilities clean and attractive. The physical environment of your facility or practice area must be considered for its maximum use and aesthetic appeal. Like new uniforms, an attractive and colorful practice room can motivate athletes.

Don't neglect other areas like the weight room, the school hallways, and conference room (where the athletes watch game videos). All of these rooms should be cleaned and organized before you use them for practice. Either accomplish this yourself or turn in work orders for the custodians.

If necessary, use the off-season to clean, paint, and polish. Consider every area where athletes practice or meet, including the practice room, locker room, weight room, classroom, etc. Use volunteer players and parents to assist you with this. Put up championship banners, signs with the school logo and colors, framed pictures of all-state athletes, and motivational slogans. Consider the lighting, floors, and lockers as well. Be sure they are bright, clean, and repaired where needed.

Athletes appreciate and enjoy facilities like this, and their personal motivations increase when they detect that the athletic department and their coaches are concerned about the areas where they practice and compete. Accomplishing this may take extra time, effort, and funds, but these expenditures are worth it.

#7: Design a Team Poster/Calendar

Today's coaches have to realize that their work isn't completed after practice has ended. An added duty that too many coaches leave unattended is publicizing their program. Effective public relations can have a significant influence on team success and the athletes' motivation. One way to achieve this is by designing and distributing a team poster/calendar.

The team poster/calendar should have pictures of the team and possibly individual players (if it is a small squad), the season schedule, the school logo and/or mascot, and where and how to buy tickets. One coach at a rural school placed a picture of his players dressed in hunting gear above the caption: "We're in the Hunt for a Championship." Another coach had his wrestlers wear leather and sit on motorcycles. The looks on their faces told me they were truly motivated.

Post the team poster/calendar in the school, community businesses and stores, athletes' homes, and city hall. Once community members and parents are aware of competition dates and see the faces of the players, they may get more excited about the season and even encourage other potential athletes to join the team. These people can spread the word about your team to their relatives, neighbors, and friends and bring them to competitions to make a loud, strong, and united cheering section. They can add enthusiasm to the program, which in turn increases the popularity of your sport in the school system and the motivation of your players.

Public relations and advertising are closely connected here. You are a salesman, and your product is your program. Your objective is to attract the attention of the people in your school and community and get them interested in your product. This has become a principal way to motivate athletes. An assistant principal at Oak Harbor (OH) High School lists the following among the job requirements when hiring a coach: "the right attitude to work with the community, relate well to students and parents, and some experience in public relations."

Gaining support from an entire community is certainly challenging and, to be sure, often slowly accomplished. Yet, do not be surprised by a snowball effect after you begin your efforts. Your own passion for your program can serve to inspire others to support it and your players. Fostering enthusiasm for your team in both the school and general community may appear to be an overwhelming challenge, but this responsibility cannot be neglected, especially if you want to motivate your athletes.

#8: Design a Media Guide

Another public relations method to motivate players is to design, develop, and distribute a media guide for the local media and community.

A typical media guide provides the following information:

- Facts about the school—address; phone numbers; nickname; colors; and enrollment numbers
- Facts about the school's athletic affiliations—conference; district or region; division; and state
- List of school administrators—superintendent, principal, assistant principal(s), athletic director, school board president and members, and dean(s) of students
- Name of booster club president and officers
- School logo
- Preview of the coming season
- Schedule
- Profile of the head coach and assistant coaches, including middle school coaches
- Team roster, beginning with senior athletes. Include a picture of each senior and a photograph of the entire squad
- Brief history of the program
- List of team record holders
- Conference championships—year by year
- Sectional championships—year by year
- District/state championships—year by year
- Regional placers and champions—year by year
- Qualifiers to the state tournament—year by year—including state placers and champions
- Team championships—conference, tournaments
- Profiles of other personnel, including managers, statisticians, trainers, and cheerleaders

Conclude the media guide with an overview of the high school—its academic and other extracurricular programs (drama, student government, etc.), the composition of its student body, and its reputation for excellence. You can also provide on a back page some informative details about the sport—the scoring, for example—and how athletes qualify for the state tournament.

The intent again is publicity and motivation. To design this media guide seek help from any school-related personnel, especially those persons involved in graphics and computers, and have it ready for distribution at the beginning of the season. The parents of your athletes will be impressed with your efforts and the athletes themselves will be motivated by the professional and serious approach you take to the program and their previous accomplishments.

2

Early in the Season

#9: Show Enthusiasm

Clearly, you have to enjoy coaching and working with athletes. You show this with enthusiasm, or a display of eagerness, intensity, and zeal. The athletes, in turn, should recognize your excitement and self-confidence and feel compelled to match your energy and attitude. Enthusiasm can often prompt athletes to believe in you, especially through those difficult periods (losses), because you appear unmoved by a setback. Therefore, create an enthusiastic atmosphere in the practice room and the locker room so that the athletes know you are concerned for their welfare and passionate about their success.

Your enthusiasm prompts athletes to act on their own personal motivations. Furthermore, this type of motivation is closely linked to emotion.

#10: Develop Team Pride

Don't expect every athlete to come out for your team at the beginning of the season with a perfect positive attitude, eager to learn, excited about success, and ready to work hard. Motivate them by speaking about team and individual pride. You have to nurture a winning attitude and pride in the program. Employ the following strategies to develop team pride.

- Be sure each athlete knows his value to the team.
- Point out how the team has succeeded in the past.
- Use terms like *"Our* team . . ." and *"We*'re on track . . ."
- Highlight team accomplishments.
- Regularly discuss the team's goals.
- Show them trophies, banners, or videos that prove your success in previous seasons.
- Frequently refer to the team logo/nickname, school colors, and school name.

#11: Avoid Coercion

Read what several athletes have to say about this issue:

- "I don't get motivated by coaches who are always angry. They have to be fun at times, and they have to be a friend."

- "To motivate me, the coach has to be able to give constructive criticism and encouragement, not sarcasm."

- "He should talk in an encouraging manner instead of yelling. He should only talk positive."

The point here is that you must never use physical coercion or verbal threats as a motivator. These methods only demonstrate how important team success is for you, not the athletes. In the short term, you could increase their efforts in practice, but in the long term you will only make them bitter and tense about competing.

After competitions, many coaches favor a brief lecture in the locker room or on the bus in which the match is analyzed and performances discussed, especially if the results were below expectations. However, after any competition, especially one that has been rigorous or disappointing, the athlete cares little for any commentary. If you must do this, make it only a quick, objective analysis of the competition and make only positive comments. Remember, if they've performed badly they'll know it. Use this moment only to remind them of the next day's schedule (the time of practice or the next match) and to congratulate the performance of any individual(s). Remain positive after a competition (and prompt the kids to stay positive, too).

Over time you'll get better results if you praise and reward rather than criticize and punish. Remember to be realistic about your expectations of your athletes. If any part of your motivation includes a promised reward for a victory—a pizza dinner, for example—then be sure to follow through on it promptly.

Coaches must be attentive to the ways they treat their athletes during practices and matches, especially after a loss. Many of today's coaches may have grown up in an era where their coaches used discipline and punishment to motivate athletes, but that style is rarely tolerated today. According to William Beausay, president of the Academy of Sports Psychology International in Columbus, Ohio, coaches who intimidate or threaten athletes should not be allowed to continue coaching. Beausay also points out that today's young athletes won't tolerate abusive coaches because they are much more independent than their counterparts in previous decades.

When coaches physically or mentally abuse their athletes, their behavior "borders on pathological," says Frank Smoll, a professor of psychology at the University of Washington. Smoll feels that the more effective coaches utilize a liberal amount of rewards, reinforcements, and praise as opposed to those who lean toward punitive measures to influence their players' performances.

In summary, basketball coach Jerry Tarkanian says, "Yelling doesn't win ball games. It doesn't put any points on the scoreboard. And I don't think words win ball games all the time. Players do. Preparation does."

#12: Show Approval

All athletes want to know if they are pleasing the coach, both in practice and at competitions. Many (even successful athletes who, for example, have won state championships) constantly need feedback about their progress and their performance.

Routinely provide specific information about performances (practice or competition) to athletes, especially the ones who have set their own training goals. This constant assessment (beyond generic commentary like "You did a nice job today" or "You had a good practice") encourages athletes to set personal standards for their practice and, hence, the competition. Better, more specific, compliments would be, "You never stopped hustling during drills today. You're setting a standard I'd like everyone to follow. Well done!" or "Your form and follow-through on your jump shot is excellent. Do it that way all the time and no one will stop you from scoring."

In fact, players should be given some indication of their improvement after each practice. At issue here is the type of praise you give athletes. Know when to praise a little and when to praise a lot. You need to recognize that too much praise lessens the impact, value, and sincerity of your message. Concentrate on specific praise, which promotes independent action, when individuals deserve it and use generic praise to prompt the entire team to act in a certain manner.

#13: Congratulate

Simply put, start by congratulating each athlete for choosing to participate in your sport; then keep on congratulating them as the season progresses by finding as many opportunities and reasons to do so. Congratulate any positive scrimmage results, exceptional behavior, and/or diligent effort (i.e., hustle). Moreover, you can congratulate improvement and wins to motivate your athletes.

Keep in mind that how you congratulate them at the beginning of the season should probably differ from the words used near the middle or end of the season. Your athletes may see the praise as insincere if it resembles what they have heard all along (i.e., you sound more like a broken record than a pleased coach). Also, know when to offer congratulations to the team and when only certain individuals deserve it. Just be sure they know why they are being congratulated when you do so.

#14: Promote Team Leaders

Discover and then promote team leaders. But keep in mind that these athletes don't necessarily have to be captains. The truth is that during any practice or competition athletes look to their peers for leadership as much as they do their coaches. In fact, the best team leaders, or team captains, are in a way an extension of the coaching staff. They help determine the team's goals and share the responsibilities of team management and motivation.

Effective team leaders may not be the ones who lift the most weight on the bench press or yell the loudest during drills, but they often earn the most respect and show the most dependability. Such athletes arrive early for practice ready to learn and often stay afterward to master a technique. They never complain when problems occur and remain positive about the outcome of any contest. Both the coach and the team can count on such an athlete.

At the beginning of the season, seek out two to three athletes who have a take-charge attitude and a high level of commitment. They are usually veterans who believe in the program and understand and respect your coaching philosophy. Ask them privately if they'd be interested in serving as team leaders, but clarify that this request is only exploratory, not a final decision. Plus, they should feel no pressure to accept this offer.

A private discussion is best because if you thrust leadership on any individual (e.g., the kid who had the best record the previous season) the results could be disastrous. This action could cause this athlete to experience too much pressure, and he may resent you for it. You might offer leadership status to an individual on a temporary basis and decide together afterward if you both are satisfied.

One week of practice is usually adequate to identify those athletes who have the potential to serve as captains. They've been punctual, coachable, and reliable. In short, they are highly motivated and set the example younger athletes should emulate.

Announce to the team during that week that the coaches are looking for team leaders and expect several athletes to show an interest. Explain the entire selection process to the team so there are no misunderstandings or surprises. The next step is to ask them on the chosen day to declare in front of their teammates their desire to be captains. The most successful captains want to be leaders! At the end of the practice have each athlete stand and announce his reasons for wanting to be a captain. It is possible that other candidates could surface at this time or that an original choice could change his mind. After these one- to two-minute speeches, the team votes on paper ballots, which are tabulated later by the coaching staff. If the squad is large (e.g., more than 50 athletes), then three or four captains is acceptable. Smaller teams need only one or two captains. Keep in mind that too many captains can adversely affect team unity and motivation, while a single leader could set up an autocracy that could make some athletes feel uncomfortable and unmotivated.

It could happen that the team selects an athlete you deem unworthy, but you must never interfere with the balloting. The trust you have from the athletes and the acceptance the new captains need from them could be ruined if you do this. Indeed, you may ruin the motivation you are trying to create.

Announce the captains at the beginning of the next practice and meet with the new captains afterward. At this meeting, explain that you are in partnership with them, that your primary goal is to empower them and the team to compete successfully, and that you expect them to be coachable. They should work to see both themselves and their teammates improve. Be sure they have a clear understanding of their responsibilities, which include:

- Recruiting more athletes into the sport
- Helping maintain discipline in the locker room
- Leading by example
- Eliminating any hazing of younger athletes
- Leading the warm-up before practices and matches
- Helping determine strategy for the next opponent
- Deciding the uniform to be worn (if you have several) for a competition
- Communicating effectively with their teammates and the coaching staff at all times
- Addressing any grievances with the coaches
- Occasionally running practice

Give these captains meaningful responsibilities and include them in matters that involve disciplinary measures. Moreover, avoid treating them as servants. Allow them, in fact, opportunities to address teammates ("Captains' Talks") either before or after practices. After the first meeting with the team leaders, the coaching staff can finalize all plans for the coming season.

Continue to monitor the new captains. Remind them to show genuine interest in other athletes' welfare to make them feel they are not just another spoke in the wheel on the team.

If, during the season, a team leader looks like a champion one day and a chump the next, discuss the situation with him. For erratic performers like this, the underlying problem often is an intense fear of not measuring up, either in competitions or as a leader. Serving as a team leader may have expanded a feeling of pressure for them and hindered their motivation. You can lessen this pressure by pointing out their successes in contests and their positive influences on the younger athletes. Clarify your interest in their effort, not their wins and losses.

Finally, make sure your staff is prepared to work with these team leaders during the season. Each coach should know the captains' responsibilities and respect their position as leaders. In this way, the team leaders can feel confident and motivated. When you demonstrate confidence in them, you discover the power of using team leaders, and your goals for the season are successfully completed more often.

#15: Establish Rules

For any team to be successful a group effort is required and group rules are needed. The individual athlete, therefore, becomes responsible to the group, and rarely are athletes motivated when rules are either vague or ignored.

Researchers indicate that when rules are perceived as a way to punish, they only serve to pressure athletes, not motivate them. Effective rules, on the other hand, get athletes ready to handle the stress of competition. These rules are seen as a positive, almost beneficial influence in the athlete's life. Stephan Terebienic competed in varsity football and wrestling at St. Edwards (OH) High School, where he earned an individual state wrestling title. He credited his success to coaches who were "tough, strict, and demanding." Disciplined athletes are easy to coach because they follow team and school rules and make themselves accessible to instruction

The establishment of rules is part of psychological conditioning. Every time any kind of group comes together, rules and guidelines need to be established. Use the following techniques with your players:

- Begin psychological conditioning on the first day of practice
- Explain what behavior is acceptable and what isn't
- Reward behavior that leads to successful performances
- Get the athletes to believe that the rules are important
- Modify inappropriate behavior individually but stress that you are most interested in what is best for the team and the program.

Rules are simply the standards by which the group is going to operate, and sometimes the size of that group determines these standards. Consider for a moment the coach who trains five athletes and the coach who trains 50. They will have different responsibilities for their athletes and different needs, though each has to consider if their rules are just means to maintain order, if they are to restrict unwanted behavior, or if negative consequences apply only to certain actions.

Former NFL coach Bud Grant says: "When making decisions, there are three things you have to watch out for. The first is that you can never be afraid of what the critics will think or say. The second is not to make decisions too soon. If you make them before you have to, you'll have a hard time changing your decision should new information become available to you. The third is that when your decision is to make a rule, you had better be prepared to enforce it. If you are not, then don't make the rule."

Differences may exist between the rules you establish for practice and those you have for competitions. Carefully develop the punishment or reward system with both the school's administration and athletes' parents in mind.

What kind of rules do you need? You must of course follow sport-specific rules (like no fouling in basketball), but you need additional guidelines for players to follow that govern their behavior and conduct as members of your team. These may include:

- Attendance and punctuality at meetings, practice, and competitions, especially when transportation to another site is involved
- Caring for uniforms and equipment and replacing any lost or damaged equipment
- Being cooperative with teammates and coaches
- Displaying acceptable behavior at practice and during competition, and respecting all coaches, teammates, officials, opponents, and other school personnel
- Treating locker room facilities with respect (home and away)
- Being attentive to instructions
- Getting a coach's permission before exiting practice or leaving the site of a competition
- Abstaining from all nonprescription drugs, alcohol, and tobacco (all types).
- Reporting any injury immediately to a coach.

Other rules mandated by the athletic department, especially those about academic eligibility, must also be adhered to. When athletes respond in a disciplined fashion, they should be rewarded. When they don't, their actions need to be addressed: How have those actions hurt the team, the athlete, or the coach? The player deserves an explanation, but a goal-oriented team deserves to have any distractions removed. "The coach should always have control and the attention of his team," says Gavin Peterson, who played on three varsity teams for University (HI) High School. "A coach should always stress discipline. He should not only make his players better players but also better people at the same time."

When players violate team rules, the coaching staff must be prepared to administer consequences. Never use a physical activity as a form of punishment. If you use, for instance, sprints at the end of practice, it is possible that the players will then equate sprints, which are an effective form of conditioning, with punishment and never run them with intensity. The same holds true with any other physical activity. One coach made his athletes compete in 10 to 12 extra wrestling matches after practice if they got caught chewing gum in school, which made them stop chewing gum and start hating matches.

Instead, design consequences to not only benefit the athlete but also the entire team. The following activities can be performed if an athlete has violated a team policy:

- Mop and clean the locker room
- Pick up any trash in the workout room, gym, and locker room
- Scrub and disinfect equipment

- Clean the training room floor, tables, and equipment
- Clean a classroom

If an athlete still does not change his behavior or actions you would be wise to have a conference with him and his parents. Violations cannot be allowed to continue. These kinds of disruptions hinder everyone's opportunity and motivation to achieve success.

"Don't be afraid to remind any players who are out of line or not in the spirit of your training rules that they owe it to the school to straighten themselves out," says Paul Brown, former NFL coach and general manager. "You win when everyone works together as a team—never let one or two players pull your whole team down."

In short, establish rules for the good of the team, and then follow them. Keep in mind when you devise your rules that the punishment you have should be based on the behavior, not on the individual involved. Regardless of the scope of the violation, rules have to be handled fairly, consistently, and as soon after the infraction as possible.

During the course of the season, you may have to deal with stealing, fighting, the use of obscenities, lost equipment, and lack of effort. Positive reinforcement for following rules often works better than negative reinforcement when rules are violated. These rules (and how they affect your athletes' motivation) should be evaluated as the season progresses.

#16: Post Slogans

Putting motivational slogans and sayings on the walls of the locker room and practice room can potentially inspire some athletes, especially during practice. Feeling exhausted at the mid-point of practice, they may look up, see Vince Lombardi's "Fatigue makes cowards of us all" on a poster board, and fight through their exhaustion to finish practice strongly. In fact, the more slogans you can place on the wall, the better.

Examples include the following:

- "The difference between the possible and the impossible lies in the man's determination." – *Tommy Lasorda*
- "Do not let what you cannot do interfere with what you can do." – *John Wooden*
- "We're good because we work harder than anybody else." – *Walter O'Malley*
- "In order to succeed greatly, you have to sacrifice greatly." – *Mike Pruitt*
- "You've got to believe deep inside yourself that you're destined to do great things." – *Joe Paterno*
- "The most certain way to succeed is to always try one more time." – *Thomas Edison*

The Edge by the late Howard Ferguson offers hundreds of quotes from all types of athletes and famous individuals that relate to success in athletics. Ask a sign company or your school art department to put them on boards that can then be nailed into the walls of your workout area. Explain some of the background of each of the individuals who stated the quotes and encourage your players to read them each day. Short, direct, and provocative statements are the most motivating, but any type of motivational slogan can be effective.

#17: Have a "Meet the Team" Night

Host a "Meet the Team" event at the beginning of the season, during the week before the first game. Invite program athletes, managers, statisticians, coaches, administrators, fans, faculty, the media, students, and parents.

Most parents are pleased when their child decides to join an interscholastic sport, and they are even more pleased when they can see and hear him acknowledged in front of his peers. The "Meet the Team" event, best held on a weekday evening, accomplishes this and motivates players.

A typical agenda for this event should take no more than one and a half hours. You, as the head coach, should do the following:

- Welcome those who attend and thank them for their recognition of the importance of the "Meet the Team" event.
- Introduce the managers and acknowledge them for their daily contributions to program.
- Have the advisor to the statisticians introduce these individuals and clarify their duties during games.
- Introduce your coaching staff and give the important background details of each coach. Allow each coach to say a few words, if he is comfortable speaking to a large group.
- Explain the coaching staff's philosophy, goals, and expectations for each squad—the freshmen, junior varsity, and varsity. You should also explain your expectations of parents, which usually centers on the kind of behavior they should display in the stands (sportsmanship, enthusiasm, etc.).
- Comment briefly on typical practice activities. You want to invite the parents to an actual practice.
- Display a slide show or videotape of the athletes in action in practice or at a scrimmage.
- Allow a few guest speakers to make presentations to the parents and athletes. Some possibilities include a sports psychologist, physical therapist, college coach or athlete, a licensed nutritionist, and an experienced mother of an athlete.
- Invite the athletic director or principal to speak to the group.
- Distribute an information packet that includes the practice and competition schedule, nutrition guide, and training rules.
- Introduce, in order, the freshmen, junior varsity, and varsity teams, or organize the introduction by classes, beginning with freshmen and ending with seniors. Possibly allow the team captains to make a brief comment on their expectations for the season.

- Conclude by thanking the fans and parents and offering your hope that the season will be a pleasant and memorable experience for them. Invite everyone to stay for any informal discussions and refreshments (ask some parents to arrange this for you).

The bottom line is that athletes enjoy being first introduced and then publicly praised by their coaches. They may feel even more motivated when they see parents, administrators, and others recognizing the importance of their participation in the sport. The "Meet the Team" event can begin the season on a positive note and send some motivational messages.

#18: Create a Display Case

Use color, pictures, the team logo, and player's names when designing a display case that can help motivate athletes. You should display your players and their accomplishments for all to see. Hopefully, you can utilize a display case in a prominent and well-traveled area of the school.

Ask art students or the art teacher to assist you in making the display colorful—featuring your school colors—and bright. Feature the athletes' pictures and the team roster, the school logo, and your competition schedule.

As the season progresses, post news articles about your team and additional pictures, trophies, and/or banners. Some coaches put Athlete of the Week Awards, motivational slogans, team T-shirts, and small banners in a display case to highlight their team and motivate their athletes. One quick warning: Be cautious about overloading a small case or neglecting any member of the team.

#19: Plan a Retreat

Though you and your administration may worry about supervision, you can develop team unity, friendship, and motivation while on a retreat. You can arrange this for any season of the year, depending on your personal schedule and goals. In the summer, some coaches take their teams camping and canoeing while others have a picnic and a softball game. A strong sense of fellowship is established within the team, and the kids and the coaches strengthen their rapport. When arranging this activity, be sure parents and administrators are clearly informed about all plans.

3

All Season

Elsa/Getty Images

#20: Communicate

Good coaching requires good communication. Always consider how you transmit messages and how athletes interpret them. What gets in the way of effective communication and, in turn, effective motivation?

- Poor verbal skills by the coach
- Athletes who don't pay attention
- Athletes who don't understand verbal cues
- Messages that are inconsistent
- An environment that threatens open dialogue

Most breakdowns of communication occur when coaches tell their athletes what they're doing wrong. In fact, these instances are often characterized by statements like, "C'mon, try again. Do it right," "What's wrong with you?" "That's not how to do it," or "C'mon, *think*."

Instead, you will get better results by providing exact information about the correct technique or behavior, such as "Be sure you push off the starting block" instead of "You gotta get outta there faster!" You should always be more concerned with teaching than judging, especially with those athletes who may already have low self-esteem. When athletes hear judgmental language they often become tense and uneasy, even defensive, and certainly less motivated. Any worries they may have about reaching their goals become magnified.

The degree of motivation may vary from athlete to athlete, but each one is entitled to the same acceptance, respect, and concern. Each athlete deserves your complete attention when he communicates. Most often, the better the coach communicates, the more motivated the athletes will be.

Allow players to communicate as well. Invite them to provide input into any plans for the program, and then discuss the contribution they want to make. By doing this, you are both setting up open communication and fostering their commitment.

Whether your means of communication is accomplished through personal conferences or team discussions (you should do both), the athletes need to see that you are articulate, concerned, and specific when you talk. You show that you are articulate when you choose your words carefully. You demonstrate concern when you speak more about their health, family, and academics than their athletic performances. Finally, athletes understand you better when your comments are specific and direct.

#21: Listen

Effective motivation stems from effective communication, but communication must be more than talking. You also have to listen and comprehend. The athlete needs to see that your desire to communicate equals your level of concern. When communicating, you must be an effective listener. This means that you give adequate time to hear what the athlete wants to say.

As he talks you should focus intensely on what he says and repeat the message as you understand it to see if your understanding is correct. Also, never interrupt the athlete. For example, an appropriate response could be "What I hear you saying is . . ." followed by your recollection of the athlete's comments. Regardless of what he says, hold back any emotional or judgmental response.

Be an active listener, as opposed to a passive, silent listener. In active listening, you interact with the athlete by providing him with a paraphrased response that proves you understand what he has said. And don't neglect those physical mannerisms that make up nonverbal communication; head and hand movements, gestures, touching, body position, even the tone of your voice are all associated with any act of verbal communication.

#22: Show Respect

Each athlete, regardless of his talent, ability, or skills, whether he routinely struggles in competitions or often achieves victory, deserves your total respect. Remember the old saying: To get respect you have to show respect. The importance of respecting each athlete's personal motivations and abilities cannot be overstated.

Would *you* work hard for a coach if you did not feel he respected you? Probably not. Use the term *respect* often when you dialogue with your athletes and be sure they understand what it means.

Pay particular attention to the athletes who are junior varsity. They are as important to any program as the superstars. Certainly they have to learn to "pay their dues," but they should be treated with as much attention and respect as the varsity.

Furthermore, no athlete deserves mediocre attention from the coach. Spend some time with each athlete during each practice and/or school day, and develop a system involving the entire coaching in which the coaches acknowledge each player each day (e.g., four coaches, 40 players—each coach makes sure to have some contact with 10 players each day). If an athlete needs to talk, make time to meet with him. When an athlete recognizes that the events in his life and the concerns he has matter to you, you increase his level of motivation to your sport.

#23: Show Fairness

Along with respect, fairness is a very important trait for a coach to have. All athletes, even professionals, want to know their coaches are being fair with them. Athletes' motivation lessens if they feel the coach's decisions are either arbitrary or self-serving. The first step to showing fairness is establishing the standards by which the team is to operate and the second step is to adhere to those standards.

Don't grant some athletes time off, for example, if you refuse the same request from others. Don't give some athletes special privileges unless *all* athletes have the opportunity to earn them. And don't highlight or praise the same players repeatedly. In each case, it may seem you are doing something positive for your athletes, but in actuality you are showing a lack of fairness.

In short, treat athletes consistently and fairly.

#24: Be Organized

You've heard the old cliché: Failing to plan is planning to fail. This statement is especially appropriate to the coaching profession. "No matter how naturally gifted an athlete or team may be, the coach without a plan for the development of those talents will usually fail to unlock their full potential," says Geoff Gowan, former national track and field coach for England, Puerto Rico, and Canada. An Ohio high school principal adds: "When I hire a coach I look for someone who has a concern for students and good coaching skills, and I especially consider their organizational skills."

Before beginning any activity that involves a group that is directed toward a certain goals, you need to get organized. Athletes are motivated in part by a coach who is organized and on task. Your organizational duties include:

- Arranging a daily practice schedule
- Getting directions for all away competitions (to distribute to parents)
- Arranging for guest clinicians or coaches
- Doing an inventory of uniforms and equipment (use your athletic department's Supplies Request Form to order necessary equipment)
- Arranging for scrimmages with other schools
- Arranging for games to be videotaped by a parent or assistant coach
- Determining and designing Player of the Week Awards (a T-shirt, certificate, trophy, etc.)
- Consulting with your athletic director about his expectations for the team and the use of the school facilities throughout the season

Whether you coach a YMCA team or a Division I college program, the obligations and functions for proper team management are the same. Athletes require and deserve a structured and disciplined approach by the coach. Preparations and practices cannot be arranged haphazardly. Your players need to know what to expect and how to respond to the activities the coaching staff plans. The athletes are motivated in this scenario because they see an organized coach as the catalyst to help them realize their potential.

The time allotted for practice, the competition schedule, and the length of the season can determine the activities you plan for your athletes. Consider these important fundamentals:

- Every practice needs to have specific objective(s).
- Athletes need to know clearly the reasons for accomplishing those objectives.
- Practice should never be punishment.

- Unless injured, all athletes should be participating at all times during practice.
- Practice should be an enjoyable and challenging experience.

Former NFL head coach Chuck Knox commented on the need for organization quite effectively: "Always have a plan and believe in it. Nothing good happens by accident—it happens because of good organization. There must be a plan for everything and the plan will prevent you from overlooking little things. By having that plan, you'll be secure and self-doubts will never become a factor."

John Wooden is even more succinct: "Without organization and leadership toward a realistic goal, there is no chance of realizing more than a small percentage of your potential." Effective organization not only gives a foundation and a sense of direction for your program, it also provides motivation.

#25: Promote Academics

One athlete says, "I'm motivated when I know that the coach is concerned about me as an athlete and as a student. He has to be straightforward with you and not feed you some line. He has to look out for you but not pamper you. When I came out of middle school, I was the top dog and I kind of had a big head. My coach set me straight and got me going in the right direction. He also let me know that there was more to life than football."

Karol Stewart, whose son competed on the varsity golf and wrestling teams in high school, says, "I think the coaches should help him build his skills, but they better keep his training and studies in a proper perspective. I think the coaches should reaffirm what his father and I have been trying to tell him all along about his academics."

"A coach has to model a strong work ethic," says one Ohio middle school principal, "and he has to promote scholarship in the classroom."

Clearly, if a coach wants motivated athletes, he must support the athlete's academic obligations and even assist him with any of his subjects if the coach is able. The athletes, their parents, and your administrators all need to know that you are concerned about each athlete's academic standing.

Always remember that the athlete's performance in the classroom is much more important than his results in competitions. Therefore, you should be especially attentive to each player's academic standing and assist those who are struggling with tutoring or time off and rewarding those who are earning high grades. Your athletes will be motivated by such efforts.

You might also consider setting up a "Study Table" where athletes gather before practice to complete homework or review for tests. A weekly or bi-weekly progress report could be arranged for any athlete you believe is doing poorly in the classroom. If problems (low grades, missing assignments, etc.) do occur, you can respond to them promptly with a tutoring session or time off from practice.

#26: Challenge the Athletes

Athletes get motivated when the coach can give them challenging yet realistic incentives to practice hard and compete aggressively. New challenges are then offered each time a task has been completed.

Improvement and accomplishment are two keys to this method of motivation. Athletes must see each practice first as a challenge to improve their skills and, second, as another step toward success. They should sense, for instance, by the end of each practice that they have met that day's challenge and taken another step toward achieving their personal goals. They should recognize that their work that day is completed, leaving them confident about their skills and eager for the next practice session.

Athletes reach their potential faster when they are challenged by the coaches, when they are pushed by their drill partner, or when their abilities are stretched at practice each day. In some respects, each practice is itself a competition. Practices should be designed, therefore, to empower athletes to experience achievement while allowing for mistakes, corrections, improvement, and finally success. If your practices accomplish this, then your athletes will stay motivated.

"I'm motivated when I'm pushed beyond my limits," says one athlete. "I like competing because it brings out the best in everyone. My coaches have encouraged me to strive to be the best."

Motivation in pressure situations also needs to be addressed. Preparing for competition is seldom fun for athletes because it involves extensive physical and mental effort. Make practice more appealing by placing the athletes in situations that lead to them being successful and build their confidence.

You can capitalize on the athletes' intrinsic motivation by challenging them to learn new techniques, avoiding punishment if they fail to master them, and instead tolerating those mistakes as natural to any learning process. Work to eliminate those errors through drill sessions and instruction. Your personal expectations for each athlete also have much to do with his level of motivation. You certainly should challenge them, but have reasonable expectations as well.

#27: Set Daily Goals

Typically, daily goals in athletics are often associated with mastering certain techniques or performing specific skills. That said, express them in simple terms. The coaching staff must do their best to enable *all* players to master that technique or skill. Players are motivated by any form of accomplishment, even if it is mastering the correct way to step on a blocking drill or sinking 10 free throws in a row.

Announce the goal at the beginning of the practice or competition. For example, "Today everyone has to show he can hit a curveball. Our pitchers are only going to throw curveballs, and I'm confident that within the hour you all will be able to hit one." Or, "We are going to end this game today without a single penalty called against us. No offsides, no illegal blocks, no illegal motion—we will not see a single yellow flag dropped because of something we did."

Each practice must have a goal, an objective the coaching staff mandates beforehand that the team has to accomplish. That goal has to be addressed with the team at the outset, and by the end of practice that goal hopefully should be achieved. Former Iowa University wrestling coach Dan Gable, whose Hawkeye teams won 15 Division I national championships, states that, "In every practice session you need to emphasize the areas that give you trouble and drill in those areas. It is important that you feel some self satisfaction after every practice."

Avoid announcing too many daily goals—one to three is enough per day. If you have too many and fail to accomplish one or two, then frustration can set in and lessen the athletes' motivation. Achieving even a single goal, however, can build confidence and, in turn, motivation.

#28: Set Weekly Goals

When athletes are informed of the goals for the week they feel both a sense of direction and purpose. They will be especially motivated if they are allowed to participate in creating the goals. You could, for instance, ask after Saturday's game or at the beginning of Monday's practice what they feel the team needs to work on. Maybe they're disappointed by their field goal percentage or their times in the last track meet. If so, ask them to state purposeful goals for the week (e.g., "increase our field goal percentage by 20%" or "reduce our relay times by at least 30 seconds overall" or "learn ten more takedowns in our next match").

Be sure that these goals are stated in specific terms (not "Let's shoot better" or "We need to get in better shape"), that they are measurable, and that they are achievable. Athletes are first motivated when they are reminded each day of the weekly goals and again if they achieve them.

#29: Set Seasonal Goals

Ladd Holman, a former head wrestling coach at Delta (UT) High School whose teams won 23 state titles, had a simple formula for success that involved following a sequence of steps:

- Set a specific goal for the season
- Decide what needs to be sacrificed to reach the goal
- Work hard enough to achieve the goal

Like the coming attractions for a movie, a seasonal goal is something the athletes can see to use to build excitement and motivation. If designed correctly, seasonal goals keep everyone on the same path and headed in the same direction. Often these are phrased in terms like "win the league," "make it to the state playoffs, or "go undefeated," but these seasonal goals could have nothing to do with winning. They could, for instance, promote team camaraderie (no one quits), academics (everyone has a 2.5 GPA or better), or rules (no one breaks training rules).

Goals first need to be created by the team as a whole. Second, they should focus on what the athletes can *do*. Finally, they should be phrased in terms of positive outcomes. For example, the first goal below is phrased incorrectly, while the second expresses the goal in a more positive way:

- We will not commit any penalties against this high school.
- We will wrestle a penalty-free match against this high school.

Put goals in terms of what you want the athletes to do. For example, a team goal may be to decrease relay times by 15% by the end of the season or to increase the total amount of poundage on the bench press. Avoid goals like "dominate our opponents" or "do our best," which are vague and immeasurable.

The competitions early in the season can be considered intense training sessions, valuable learning experiences, and stepping stones to the tournaments at the end of the season. Unfortunately, too many coaches feel threatened by early-season losses and too many athletes see them as indicators of their entire season. The more important goals reflect what the individual athletes and the coaching staff want to accomplish by the *end* of the season. Everything before that should be seen as competitive training sessions that offer valuable experiences.

Emphasize to your athletes the importance of establishing goals and, of course, involve them in the formation of those goals. They need to see that goals are helpful, that they add a competitive challenge (motivation) for the squad, and prompt a better work ethic.

Meaningful season goals for coaches should include:

- Making the health of the athletes a priority
- Educating the athletes about the value of hard work, cooperation, self-discipline, and commitment
- Promoting an enjoyment of the sport
- Empowering athletes to set individual goals
- Fostering a desire to be successful
- Demanding that the school be represented in a respectful and dignified manner
- Promoting a successful relationship with parents, the community, and the school administration
- Encouraging victory in competitions.

The coaching staff should not set all of the season goals alone. All members of the team must be involved. You can even talk to administrators and some parents and get their input. The group has to operate with one positive direction—"Be league champions"—which should be clarified either at the beginning or end of every practice until the goal has been accomplished. Your goals must be sound, reasonable, and reachable.

Be sure that every athlete feels that he is making a strong contribution to the attainment of these goals. No one, including assistant coaches, should feel that he is only along for the ride, that his input or effort doesn't really count, or that the superstars are the only ones helping the team succeed. The team's success depends on many factors, but all of your athletes certainly have to feel that they play important roles on your team. They have to see that all their effort is for a worthwhile purpose.

In short, seasonal goals are challenges. They are a means of making the coaches' and the athletes' efforts purposeful. They are essential for any program. David Hemery analyzed the importance of goals established cooperatively between the coach and players in his book *The Pursuit of Sporting Excellence*. "The mutual effort towards a common goal," writes Hemery, "brings a closeness and sharing and this enhances communication. This makes the process valuable in itself, regardless of the outcome."

Before you can discuss goals with your athletes, you need to have a more private discussion—with yourself. You need to discover the goals *you* want to accomplish—goals so important, in fact, that you will not procrastinate, relax, or quit until they are accomplished. Maintain a positive attitude and a clear focus on those goals.

"Common goals, similar attitudes, mutual respect—that's what creates a successful season," says Rex Holman, who won a national wrestling championship his senior year for Ohio State University. The same results can happen for your team if you set meaningful goals, develop an organized plan of action, and follow through with passion and diligence.

#30: Avoid Pressurized Goals

A pressurized goal resembles a statement like, "We *have* to win this one." This can work against motivation, not enhance it. You may feel that demanding a certain result (e.g., a winning season or a margin of victory of 20 points) is simply a means to challenge the athletes, but most of them will see it as pressure, which prompts tension more often than triumph.

Stress improvement, not wins or losses. If your goals surface from dialogues with all members of the team, they are not likely to be pressurized goals. Instead, goals designed cooperatively between coaches and players are far more appealing and prompt much less anxiety. If you still remain uncertain if pressure is linked to any goal, talk to your administrators or to other coaches. If it is, then make an adjustment.

The bricks that make up the foundation of the athletic program are your personal principles. These principles determine the decisions you make, the goals you and the team set, and the attitude you express each day. Be sure you don't introduce pressure to your athletes; they probably already have enough to deal with.

#31: Have Fun

Howard Ferguson, legendary Ohio wrestling coach whose St. Edwards High School teams won 10 state titles, offered this caution to coaches: "The next time you're getting ready to play a game, ask yourself why you're playing. A game is not supposed to be work. It's not something you have to do . . . Do it for fun. Do it because you want to do it. Practice is the hard part; the game should be fun . . . Stop worrying about winning and losing. If you've prepared right, you shouldn't have to worry."

Olympic swim coach James "Doc" Counsilman routinely used silly antics and obnoxious humor to make his swimming practices fun. A varsity wrestler adds: "Practice has to be fun. I want practice to raise my level of competition, but I also expect the coach to give all athletes an equal chance and help all the athletes in the same way." Develop a sense of humor and try to organize drills in practice into fun and challenging competitions, but avoid turning practice into a party.

Be sure, therefore, to add fun into the learning process. While repetition is needed in drills, learning need not be boring or dull. For example, you could, without saying a word, teach an entire practice using pantomime, charades, and gestures to make points and teach techniques. A middle school football player admits, "I keep participating when the coach makes me feel good about myself, when he makes practice fun."

Consider that hardship in practice doesn't necessarily translate into winning games. Concentrate on having fun, teaching the fundamentals, and building the self-esteem of the athletes. Your better athletes will always find a way to win regardless of the amount of emphasis that is placed on victory, and your less-skilled athletes will find the sport to be rewarding. "Sometimes I find myself getting a little too serious," admits professional tennis player Andre Agassi. "When I'm having fun it breaks the tension and I play much better."

#32: Use the Buddy System

President Franklin Delano Roosevelt said, "People acting together as a group can accomplish things which no individual acting alone could ever hope to bring about."

Having athletes work with a partner on a daily basis can contribute equally to athletes' psychological and physical development. Their motivation and self-discipline improve when they are responsible to a specific teammate, and anxiety is often lessened when burdens can be shared with a partner. If they are paired correctly, each player shares the same goals and objectives as his counterpart, which can enhance mental preparation for upcoming competitions.

Before you pair up members of your team, you should review their attitudes and goals. Partners must be mutually supportive—encouraging each other's improvement, enhancing each other's skills, and maximizing each other's conditioning. If each athlete views his partner's training as important as his own, then both perform better both in practice and in matches. Furthermore, both are more likely to recover from poor performances more quickly. In fact, research has shown that when an athlete is taught by a peer, he learns at a faster rate than when instructed under normal coach/athlete circumstances.

One type of buddy system is to have more mature senior athletes act as mentors for younger ones. Another is to link freshmen with freshmen, sophomores with sophomores, etc. The second option tends to match up players who know each other better and might, in fact, be friends outside the team. Both systems give athletes a sense of responsibility to themselves and their teammates; plus, they feel motivated to live up to their counterpart's expectations.

When the team assembles on the first day of practice, form a close circle and discuss these three questions:

* Why are you here?
* What do you want to accomplish this season?
* What is one personal item you can share with us?

This question-answer process takes about 20 to 40 minutes (depending on the size of your team) and usually involves some serious thought on their part, especially by the younger guys who may not be certain yet what they want to accomplish. After all, how often are young people asked to voice their goals to their peers. More importantly, everyone listens. As the returning lettermen speak, the newcomers learn why the sport is enjoyable and what is possible for them.

Answers, of course, will vary, but there is a common thread that connects all responses. Their answers to the first question often reflect their need to be part of a group. One study reveals that this need to socialize, called "affiliation," is the primary factor for athletes joining any particular team. Accordingly, kids seem to consider gaining friendship as more important than achieving awards. Typical responses here are, "Because my friend is on the team," "I don't like football and cross country is perfect for guys like me," and "It looks like fun."

Teenagers, by nature, are often idealistic. This becomes quite evident when they respond to question #2. You may hear the following:

- "Be champions of the conference."
- "Get in great shape."
- "Go undefeated."

Obviously, they have high expectations for the team, and from this a *group* attitude toward team success emerges. They discover that many of them have the same goal: they all want to have a winning, competitive team. The coach here can infer also that they want practices to be intense, yet enjoyable. Through their own words, they have become unified toward a common purpose and outcome: challenging practices and a successful season.

The final question may be as brief as "Where do you live?" or "What's your favorite movie?" or something more complex like "What's the craziest thing you've ever seen in this school?" or "How would you define courage?" Some good-natured teasing may occur, but humor helps ease the tension some of the athletes may feel about beginning a new season. Be sensitive, of course, to the athletes' socioeconomic and cultural backgrounds. For instance, questions about dating or parents could embarrass some kids.

Your input up to this point should have been minimal. The athletes have done all the talking, even most of the decision-making, especially in regards to team goals. You have simply directed whose turn it is to speak next.

An athlete's intrinsic motivation improves when he senses being "in control." Conversely, if he has little or no control, he tends to be less motivated. Offer them control from day one; share responsibility with them by using the buddy system.

Don't misunderstand this concept and neglect your status as team leader. You still must make many decisions in consultation with your coaching staff. However, the athletes can be involved in many issues regarding team objectives and direction, as in the following:

- Scheduling: "We have a choice of three tournaments next year. Which one would you like to compete in?"
- Motivation: "Guys, I'm not giving the pep talk today. You are. Johnny, tell Jimmy what he needs to do today to win his tennis match."

- Technique: "Jenny, show us how you set yourself before you go to spike the ball."

Drill partners should know to give minimum resistance at the beginning stages of drilling a maneuver and increased resistance through the repeated execution of that skill. This enables both athletes to gain confidence in mastering the technique and in each other. And by the first competition, the intent is for the athletes to feel responsible for the team's success and to support each other.

The results of this approach can be rewarding. Once coaches learn to share responsibility and become partners with their athletes, the kids take more pride in team success and have more at stake in team achievement. This method of coaching places more trust in the athletes, which has a positive effect on their self-esteem and motivation.

According to Mike Eruzione, center for the 1980 USA Olympic hockey team, the buddy system was especially evident on that squad. "We all came together six months before the 1980 Winter Olympics with different styles of hockey and different ethnic beliefs . . . but we made ourselves a team. Individually, we could not have done it."

#33: Be Honest

For many coaches, being straightforward with athletes can be difficult. You may fear hurting a young person's feelings or lessening their self-esteem, but if you conceal the truth from players or mislead them, you may ruin your relationship and rapport with your athletes.

It becomes a matter of integrity. If you are sincere about teaching athletes to obey the rules and compete fairly, then you must do the same. You have to be honest with them. This topic is so significant that three major Ohio colleges have semester courses for educators in ethics alone. Coaches, it seems, need training in how to be ethical and reflect honesty.

You may find it useful to address your concerns regularly throughout the season, even weekly. One varsity athlete respects his coach for speaking out. "He has also taught me how to overcome hardships," he claims, "how to take pride in the team, not to cheat ever. He's a strict coach."

If you want to be recognized for operating an honest program, you need to have strong ethics and character. The head coach needs to instruct assistants on why integrity is important. The public must see the staff as individuals who take responsibility for their actions and refuse to compromise their values, even when the issue is unpopular or winning is put in jeopardy.

Even if you are desperate to win you cannot violate ethical behavior. Cheating cheapens the value of winning; true glory comes when victory is achieved honestly and fairly.

Develop in your athletes a sense of pride in a program that functions by the rules. They have to appreciate their own integrity and honor it in their opponents. This doesn't happen easily or quickly for most teenagers, who rarely find fault ignoring authority's rules. Spend the time to explain the importance of integrity to your team. It may be a conversation you repeat often.

Honest actions must consistently be a part of your program. "Truth has no special time of its own," says Albert Schweitzer, the French physician. "Its hour is now—always." Athletes need to believe in you; they can tell when a coach isn't being honest or consistent. Respect and honesty have to go both ways.

Finally, do not offer money or gifts as rewards for the athletes' participation or performance. You need to carefully consider the incentives you provide to motivate your athletes. Their age, maturity level, interests, and culture are important here. You must be a disciplined person. Regarding ethical behavior, you are the main role model the athletes need to follow.

#34: Post Statistics

To some coaches, statistics are meaningless, with the exception of wins and losses. However, most athletes always seem to be interested in, for example, their tackles, their record, or their times. That said, the coach should post statistical charts—related to the athlete's individual performance in recent competitions and over the season as a whole—that reveal clearly the athlete's progress toward achievement.

Display these statistics on a locker room bulletin board each week, possibly daily, during the season. Do this routinely, as athletes need feedback. They get motivated by seeing objective results of their efforts in practice, especially when the statistics show improvement. Statistics can identify for athletes their strengths and weaknesses in the sport and help them get self-directed to eliminate those weaknesses. For instance, a basketball player with a lower free throw percentage than field goal percentage can often be seen staying after practice shooting at the foul line. That happens because his observation of posted statistics has motivated him to correct a weak area of his game.

#35: Involve Cheerleaders

Cheerleaders can be major source of motivation for athletes, regardless of their gender. Cheerleaders also include spirit groups, pep clubs, statisticians, and possibly the student council.

What can these groups do?

- Make posters and displays in school hallways
- Organize pep assemblies and lead cheers
- Advertise your program in the school
- Increase the attendance at your games and tournaments
- Write articles about your players for the school newspaper (or other publications)
- Make announcements about the team and top performers
- Photograph your players and highlight them in school display cases
- Put a team schedule and pictures in community businesses and stores
- Pass resolutions (student government) praising the team and/or individual performers
- Send good luck notes to the athletes

It is important to get the student body on your side because with their support the team can become even more inspired to be successful. Once you get the cheerleaders or Pep Club involved, your guidance should be minimal if each group's advisor is willing to participate in supporting your team. Attend one of their meetings, talk about your sport, and answer any questions. Then let them create their own cheers, signs, and banners. They might also provide beverages, snacks, or other treats after a game for the athletes. Later, be sure to publicly acknowledge and thank them for their efforts.

#36: Employ a Variety of Drills

It is clear that today's coaches should employ far more sophisticated training methods than were needed just 10 years ago. If the skills of the sport can become instinctive for athletes, they can perform more successfully in a competition. Experienced coaches know to use repetition in practice so their players perform more by quick reflex than delayed reaction.

The problem is that repetition is often monotonous for many athletes, prompting more lethargy in practice than enthusiasm. Therefore, keep your players motivated by employing a variety of drills and sequences. In fact, involve the players themselves in the actual technique instruction by briefly discussing with them their opinions about the techniques you plan to cover.

- "How would you block the defensive tackle from here?"

- "How would you get our opponents out of position on the serve?"

- "What am I doing wrong here? Why can't I complete my stand up?"

This type of dialogue both eliminates confusion about the purpose or skill related to a specific drill and makes athletes feel more in control of their own practice responsibilities. Question-answer session can help athletes improve their thinking skills and increase their motivation. When demonstrating techniques or strategies, you have several options:

- You can demonstrate the technique.

- A highly-skilled player can demonstrate.

- Video can be used.

- Pictures and illustrations can be used.

- You can lecture and describe the technique.

Provide various demonstrations of important techniques (often from different angles) and try to relate the new maneuver to some previously-mastered skill. A continuous dialogue between you and your players should take place while skills are being taught. By doing so, the coach can discover who can add to the explanation and who may not understand it. This keeps players active and motivated during instruction, instead of acting as passive and sluggish observers.

#37: Play Popular Music

Playing popular music during practice has both advantages and disadvantages. The key advantage is that players will probably enjoy the music and lyrics and look forward to that interval of practice when the radio or CD player is turned on. This can be done during scrimmaging, foul shooting, serving drills, and running laps. And since the players' musical tastes change regularly, obligate them to bring in the tapes or CDs they'd like to hear (they'll probably bring in the radio/CD player as well).

The key disadvantage is the extra noise, which either you or some players may not like. It's wise to have a manager stay near the radio or CD player and turn it off quickly on your command when you need everyone's attention. You also should be cautious about allowing inappropriate lyrics to be played.

Music, especially the kind that is high-energy and upbeat, can serve to motivate most athletes, and if used judiciously it can be a welcome part of any practice.

#38: Manage the Time

As the coach for the Super Bowl champion Oakland Raiders, John Madden operated under two rules: "Be on time" and "Play like hell." The importance of time cannot be overstated by any coach. This doesn't only refer to the athletes' attendance or punctuality. Effective time management also depends on the coach planning the sequence of step-by-step activities that the team needs to cover. Once you arrange these steps, you need to consider the total time you have to accomplish them and then determine how much time the team can spend on each one. You should follow an organized practice schedule each day.

Being a motivational coach also requires the skill to "manipulate time," says a varsity coach with more than 22 years of experience. "You have to have the ability to rapidly adjust practice and game plans that aren't working and paint for the kids a clear picture of what you want them to do." You especially need to understand that time belongs to everyone, not just the coach.

Sometimes, one coach's one-hour practice seems to go on for eternity while another's two-hour practice seems to end too quickly. "Practices are like classes," says former Norwalk (OH) High School athletic director Mike Grose. "In fact, practices may better prepare the students for their futures than do most classes. The competition and the practicing that take place help develop the student and lead them to success after they are out of school. That's why the coach has to be organized and knowledgeable at practice."

The length of practice should be determined based on several variables: the age of your athletes, their level of maturity, the stage of the season, their knowledge, and their physical condition. Generally, short practices are suitable for the younger athlete (eight to 12 years old), while longer ones are usually not a problem for the older, better-conditioned players.

How much time you require for practice depends also on the kind of skills you need to teach. You should anticipate the questions and difficulties the kids will have prior to the practice and develop an interesting session that gets your athletes excited and eager to participate without delays.

You keep kids motivated if you start and end practice on time and follow a schedule that leads to positive outcomes. As long as your players see the time spent at practice as time spent efficiently and productively, they will participate with punctuality and enthusiasm. Effective time management is truly related to motivation.

#39: Show Knowledge

You must project credibility and believability, meaning that you know the skills and techniques of your sport and that the kids are convinced that the techniques and strategies you teach can work for them. You must also stay in control. Be prepared for potential interruptions, annoying distractions, and unexpected questions, especially when teaching very technical skills. If you have these traits, you will be able to motivate kids to pay attention and compete with confidence.

At practice, players should look at you as the expert who knows what they need to do to win. This, therefore, involves detailed organization for each day. The athletes must respect your status as their coach. Establish your credibility as quickly as possible. Credibility is probably most important at the beginning of the season to get athletes motivated and excited. Raphael Taylor participated on the varsity football, wrestling, and track teams at Cleveland Heights (OH) High School and always checked to see if his coach "knows what's best, knows what he's doing, and knows how to go about it. I made it to States because my coach got to know me better than I know myself. He knew what I was capable of."

You can demonstrate your credibility in several ways:

- Show an effective knowledge of strategies
- Be dynamic and enthusiastic
- Remain confident in every situation
- Treat all athletes in a fair and consistent manner
- Have a history of positive team performances and/or personal success

Athletes must see you as competent enough to lead them, even willing to take risks to improve their individual performances. One veteran coach adopted a wrestling program at a high school that had rarely experienced any kind of success. His credibility came from "building a successful program at the school. I saw that I had to create an environment with a family approach. A coach has to be a leader. Demanding. Enthusiastic. A motivator. A coach in today's society must work *with* players, not be their dictator."

When you increase your athletes' knowledge base and when they know about your sport's specific techniques and strategies, they will feel more confident about competing. A varsity track athlete claims, "I'm motivated by a coach who has knowledge of the sport and is able to communicate this to us in an intense way that is still fun and interesting."

In conclusion, coaches should be students of their sport themselves. Updated textbooks, coaching clinics, top-notch videotapes, and effective dialoging with other coaches can improve coaches' understanding of their sport. According to Richard Greene, an Illinois principal, the coach has to keep learning. "The coach must first possess a thorough knowledge of the sport and be able to communicate that knowledge well. If I have to fire a coach it's usually because he or she is abusive, poorly organized, or poorly prepared in the knowledge of the game."

#40: Use First Names

At every practice every player should be acknowledged in some personal way by at least one coach, and during that dialogue the coach should use the athlete's first name.

Why? Coaching is as much about how you establish relationships and rapport with your athletes as it is the skills you teach them—probably more. Using first names prompts a more personal and attached relationship between you and the athlete, and when they hear their first names used athletes are more attentive and on task.

Since practice involves a continuous communication between coaches and athletes, enhance that communication (and motivation) by using first names as often as possible, much like a classroom teacher does. This can be done when greeting an athlete, teaching him, and even in matters of discipline. Doing so can prompt players to see you as someone who cares.

Learn even the names of your athletes' parents, their brothers and sisters, maybe even how they all spent their summer vacations. When you take an active interest in each player's family, that family takes an active interest in your program. Talk to parents after matches, during the "down" times at tournaments, and at other sporting events. As you use those brief opportunities to befriend them, allow them to get to know you. As you develop these relationships, you build motivation.

#41: Keep an Even Keel

Often, an athletic season can be described as having peaks and valleys, achievements and disappointments. You could, for instance, struggle with the disappointment associated with failing to win games, to satisfy the needs of administrators, and to accomplish goals. Maybe you will have to confront poor behavior exhibited by some of your players or worse, the loss of a key player due to injury. All these events can lessen *your* motivation and indirectly the motivation of your athletes.

That said, keep an even keel and avoid the emotional rollercoaster of the season. This will require stamina and enthusiasm on your part, plus understanding that conflicts are inevitable whenever large groups of people come together, even if they all are dedicated to the same general goal, and that no team goes undefeated forever.

Furthermore, rarely will all persons in your program have identical expectations, interests, or timetables. You must be prepared to confront criticism so that it does not affect you or the athletes' motivation. Any form of disapproval can cause even the most confident coach to feel inadequate, uncertain, or unmotivated.

Coaching is a way to contribute to young people's lives. Few adults in their lives help youngsters set goals, train them to achieve those objectives, and then reward them for their efforts. Sports offer athletes a wonderful opportunity for physical, mental, and social growth. You are the catalyst for this growth and you are probably their key motivator. This is why you need a system in place that enables you to deal effectively with the low points in a season in which problems are solved in a positive way and losses are handled so that all athletes stay motivated and on target to their goals.

First, take responsibility for solving any problem or dealing with any loss, without rationalizing or placing any blame on someone else. Second, remain patient, objective, and understanding, even if the problem is ongoing or the loss is upsetting. Third, possibly with the help of your coaching staff, come up with multiple solutions and strategies for dealing with the problem or loss. Finally, make a public commitment to solving the conflict and overcoming the loss. This leads to a more diligent endeavor on your part in handling the problem and, in turn, models the approach you want your athletes to take when they confront adversity.

Never lose control in front of your athletes or allow emotion, especially anger, to cloud your actions. Remain calm and objective, even if the problem is personal or the loss happened in the championship game. Events like this are simply part of the profession. Successful coaches never remain discouraged or indulge in self-pity.

In conclusion, reducing the emotions you attach to losing and problems and minimizing their disruptive influence are crucial to effective motivation. Understand that you don't have to win championships right away, and kids most often will forgive you for your errors if you forgive them for theirs.

As a former coach in the NFL, Sam Rutigliano has seen all the highs and lows of coaching. Currently the head football coach at Liberty University, Rutigliano sees the way to a rewarding career by finding "a middle level." He warns that "a lot of good men become Jekyll and Hydes and everyone they touch suffers." So keep an even keel. Don't get too excited about winning or too disappointed with a loss. Your athletes need to see a coach who maintains his composure and poise no matter who wins the competition.

#42: Arrange Pep Assemblies

Pep assemblies seem to be part of the environment of nearly every school in the country. Some are brief, simple affairs where players are introduced and the head coach makes a speech, while others are extravagant events involving confetti, fireworks, music, and speakers including local politicians, administrators, coaches, and team captains. Regardless of the format, well-structured pep assemblies, whether they are in the high school gym or in the football stadium, are important to the motivation of athletes.

Try to make your pep assembly as dramatic as possible. One part of the event must include introducing players, so consider unique ways to do this. For example, have basketball players in uniform emerge from the locker room through a tunnel of cheerleaders and the pep band and break through a paper hoop. Arrange for the golf team to enter an outside rally on golf carts. Cross country and track athletes (in uniform) can run in. Avoid the traditional, "Line up and step forward when I call your name" introduction. Instead, get creative in how players are introduced.

Music is very important. Play the students' favorite music during the rally from a speaker system or have the school pep band perform in between introductions. Don't worry about students dancing in the bleachers—that means they're involved and enjoying the rally. In fact, you do not want the other students just sitting passively. You want them yelling, cheering, and stomping.

To accomplish this, try to include audience participation. Male and female members of each class can be pulled from the stands to engage in various contests: Who can throw a football the farthest? Who can sink the most free throws? Who can win a game of musical chairs? Use wacky relays on tricycles, pie eating contests, and dance contests. You can even make this a Battle of the Classes.

An effective way to boost the student body's interest and educate them about your sport is to have an all-school assembly where you introduce all squad members and display athletes in action. You can use a videotape on a large screen, a slide show, or some players who demonstrate an actual contest that you choreograph beforehand.

Some pep assemblies involve skits, bonfires, and even motorcycles. The intent is not to divert attention from the athletes but to heighten the excitement in the student body about the team and the season.

Your speakers could include any of the following: school administrator(s), the mayor (or another popular politician), a professional athlete, a celebrity, the Booster Club president, and the varsity captains. All should have one focus: praise the players and wish them good luck.

Don't neglect to involve cheerleaders, the pep club, the dance team, and the marching band. You can even involve the drama club or theater department to perform skits or scenes. Just be sure all these groups are given enough advance notice.

A typical and successful rally should last 30 to 40 minutes and be fast-paced. Students and staff in the school and community members should know about it at least two to three weeks in advance through posters, flyers, and public address (p.a.) announcements. Finally, ask your athletes what they would like to have happen at the pep rally—give them some ownership, especially for their introduction, for their own motivation. They might have some great ideas.

#43: Involve Administrators

Consider yourself a "player" on the school team and the administration as the coaching staff. Once you show support for the administration's policies, they in turn can become quite enthusiastic about supporting your program and your athletes. Although many administrators are burdened by the difficulties of supervising hundreds of other teachers and students, keep your athletic director, principal, and superintendent informed about your plans and all events related to your program, both good and bad.

To motivate players, invite administrators to speak to them at practices, or possibly before a game. Ask administrators to assist with fund-raising, pep assemblies, special uniform or transportation requests, or p.a. announcements. If they're unfamiliar with your sport, teach them the strategies and the scoring. Help them understand the excitement and benefits of your sport. In short, seek their assistance in motivating your athletes.

Remember that administrators have expectations of you as well. For Richard Corbin, an administrator at Griswold (CT) Senior High School, a coach's evaluation depends on several factors. "The four key components I look for in a coach," says Corbin, "are his strength as a motivator, an innovator, a communicator, and an organizer. We want to know whether a coach hands in his paperwork on time, meets deadlines, and runs an efficient practice."

#44: Utilize Parents

Parents can be your most important support group. Indeed, you should establish a nucleus of support for your program from parents who understand and respect your coaching philosophy. "I'd not renew a coach if he or she had a communication problem with parents, students, or administrators," says Joe Webb, a former principal at Mentor (OH) High School. "A coach has to get all these people to believe in his program."

To motivate athletes, it is mandatory that you form a positive relationship with their parents. You gain parental support by being available to discuss the athlete's progress, providing technical information in simpler terms, and regularly informing them about any policies, events, or updates related to the team. A newsletter is a great communication tool. You lessen parents' questions and concerns by providing written information in which common issues are addressed (Figure 44-1). One avenue for distributing this important information is at the "Meet the Team" Night.

What can parents do for you? They can make phone calls, write letters, or talk personally to athletes who may need more motivation. They can be sure their child is getting the proper nutrition and rest. And they can attend competitions, cheer for the team, and generally support the program.

Just be careful, warns sport psychologist Jack Lesyk, Ph.D., of parents who don't know how to support the team effectively. "Sometimes adults project their own unfulfilled dreams, motivations, and goals onto their children."

Such difficulties can be eliminated often through open and candid dialogues with parents. Lesyk recommends that the coach explain to parents how to talk to their child about his feelings about competition and achievement. The coach needs to teach parents to teach their children how "to define success in terms of the attainment of their own goals" and "downplay winning and external rewards." Clearly, both the coach and parents have the same objective—a motivated athlete who is excited about competing and attentive to coaching.

Congratulations!

Your son/daughter has made an important commitment in regards to his/her decision to join the high school _____ (insert your sport name team). The coaching staff is very pleased to have your son/daughter as a member of the program, and we have organized our efforts to promote his/her individual success. _____ (insert your sport name) is a very demanding sport. It will require much effort and dedication from your son/daughter. We admire and respect him/her already for making this type of commitment.

Our Season

The season officially begins on _____ (date) and continues through _____ (date). This means, of course, we will have practices each school day and on Saturdays. Practices run from 2:45 PM to 5:15 PM (showers follow). Our competitions begin on _____ (date). I have enclosed a copy of our schedule.

Preseason Information

I expect all potential players to engage themselves in a conditioning program at the school every Monday, Wednesday, and Friday after school from 2:45-4:15 PM. They will weight train, do agility drills, and run.

Forms

Participation in _____ (insert name of sport) also involves some important forms for both the athlete and parents to complete. I have enclosed them in this envelope. Please have your son/daughter return them to me as soon as possible.

Thank you!

The coaches certainly appreciate your support in encouraging your son/daughter to compete. This is a big challenge, and we know that he/she could experience some difficulties during the season. But if we work together, your son/daughter's season can be very rewarding.

We also look forward to seeing you at our games. Parents can also order sweaters that display our school colors and name. An order form is enclosed.

Sincerely,

Figure 44-1. Letter to parents

#45: Organize Home Competitions in an Impressive Manner

One varsity athlete claims, "I'm motivated by performing well in front of a big crowd. I like being a part of the competition." Her statement emphasizes the importance of conducting home competitions in an impressive manner. You can accomplish this by employing the talents of various individuals and groups.

The first key person to involve is the athletic director. You will need his approval before making any arrangements. Confirm what is acceptable and what isn't, and do this in writing so there is no confusion about your plans for conducting the home competition in such a way that the athletes get even more motivated about competing.

The next person to consult is the audio-visual director at the school. This person can arrange music, special lighting, and staging at the competition. You may want a spotlight, for example, a certain song played during introductions, or a platform.

Ask the announcer to read a motivational script during the introduction or a list of announcements during time-outs to highlight certain players or events. Arrange for the art department to paint signs, banners, or posters to be placed in the gym or on the fence outside on the football field. Be sure, though, that these are appropriate and don't violate any guidelines related to sportsmanship.

Assistant coaches can lead specific groups of athletes onto the field or into the gym to acknowledge those players personally and allow fans to cheer for them. Also utilize cheerleaders, the marching or pep band, the pep or school spirit club, and possibly the student council to increase school spirit and attendance at the game. Ask the advisors to participate and let them determine the way they'd like to contribute. All these groups working in unison can make for an impressive showing for the fans and your players.

Finally, at home competitions it is especially important to make sure everyone has a chance to compete. Few athletes are motivated by sitting on the bench.

#46: Prepare for Failure

Teach your athletes that failure is only a word, while winning is an attitude. Everyone makes mistakes, but the better competitors don't make excuses. The very best athletes take responsibility for their losses, correct their mistakes, and move on. They don't blame others, nor do they dwell on the loss. More importantly, these athletes return to practice with an immediate incentive to improve their weak points. "It may sound strange," says Bob Richards, an Olympic gold medalist in the pole vault, "but many champions are made champions by setbacks. They are champions because they've been hurt. Their experience moved them, and pulled out this fighting spirit, making them what they are."

"The child's philosophy is a true one. He does not despise the bubble because it burst; he immediately sets to work to blow another one." The child's response to failure is perseverance, not uncertainty. In short, the child doesn't quit.

You might have athletes on your team who continually claim injuries—real or imagined, minor or major—to avoid competition and failure. To these types of athletes, the competition is more threatening than the hurt they may have. Some may actually try to become injured because only an injury can provide them some of the psychological nurturing they cannot receive elsewhere. In this way, the athlete gets sympathy, relief from the competition, attention for the injury, and possibly a heroic stature in the eyes of his peers. This is the kid who exaggerates a limp or grimaces at the slightest touch. All of these actions often are intended to cover up a lack of confidence (and motivation). In addition, he could be trying to punish himself for failing to reach a goal or live up to expectations. They are simply afraid to fail.

Try to understand both this athlete's fear of losing and his feelings of inferiority. Effective strategies would be to keep him at practice to train healthy body parts, work at weak points, and build confidence ("You're showing some real strength there, just keep doing your best"). Athletes have to realize that losing only adds weight to their lives if they let it. They can still be winners, no matter what the scoreboard indicates after the game.

Also, do not reprimand any athlete for faking an injury. If this occurs, the athlete is sending an obvious signal that a more serious problem exists below the surface, often a personal one that has nothing to do with you, the team, or the sport. Communication and understanding are the keys to straightening out this type of problem and redirecting the athlete's motivation toward having a successful season.

Be prepared to accept any athlete's anxieties about losing. According to one junior varsity basketball player, the coach has to "care and believe in everyone no matter how bad you are." A college wrestler describes his wrestling coach as "hard working. He puts kids first. He teaches what it takes to win, how to *mentally* win."

Athletes develop at different levels and times through their careers, and failure is typically part of any growth process. The key is to provide all athletes with meaningful and rewarding experiences, to help them see that losing a competition only proves what didn't work that time.

So have a pre-planned response for potential failures and examine writer Lyman Fertig's advice: "If I could have one hope for our young people as they go out into the world, it would be this: I hope they fail. I hope they fail at something that is important to them, for failure, like nothing else, is able to stimulate the right kind of person to that extra action that always makes all the difference." Fertig truly understands what you need to instill in your athletes: winning is found not on a scoreboard but in a person's character.

#47: Prepare for Excuses

Former NFL coach Don Shula states, "The superior man blames himself. The inferior man blames others." It's unfortunate, but you may see this behavior in too many of your athletes. Don't let them, however, make excuses or rationalize a defeat, and especially don't let them blame others. This is anti-motivation and can debilitate any athlete or team if allowed to continue.

Excuse-making should be anticipated and never ignored. When it occurs do not dismiss the excuse or try to make the athlete feel wrong. Instead, find out why he feels that way and seek a positive outcome. Get the complaint or issue out in the open and deal with it in a mature way, possibly in an open team discussion. The criticism that the athletes has may be fair and justified, but he must also be part of the resolution. The late college football coach Paul Bear Bryant understood this and recommended, "When you make a mistake, there are only three things you should ever do about it: admit it, learn from it, and don't repeat it."

#48: Be Ready for Injuries

Although an athlete may be injured, he need not sit out a practice session. He can still work on skills and rehabilitate the injury to remain a competitive and motivated member of the team. Rest and recovery are certainly important, but his skills (and motivation) could be reduced if he is ignored or neglected.

Unless the athlete is seriously injured he should still attend and work on skills (consult a trainer first). When an injured athlete is at practice and rehabilitating in front of his teammates, other members of the squad see him as a contributing member of the team and acknowledge him for that. In short, they are motivating each other; the healthy team members admire the injured athlete for working out despite his injury and the injured athlete doesn't feel separated from the team and unable to contribute. Coaches, however, must be cautious of the athlete who may try to do too much and further aggravate an injury. Proper supervision is crucial in these situations.

Use Figures 48-1 and 48-2 to help you plan a practice for injured athletes, depending on their type of injury.

If the athlete's ankle or knee is injured, have him perform the following upper-body exercises and drills:

- 200 sit-ups
- 200 push-ups
- Five sets of bench presses
- Five sets of dumbbell lateral raises (shoulders)
- Five sets of chin-ups or pull-ups
- Five sets of dumbbell curls
- **Basketball:** While seated, drill passing with a partner. While seated, perform 500 dribbles with each hand.
- **Baseball:** While seated, throw/catch with a partner. While seated, practice bunting.
- **Wrestling:** Practice various pinning series with a partner; practice a half-nelson vs. a partner who tries rolling.
- Lat machine pull-downs
- Personal technique instruction
- Work on grip strength for five to 10 minutes
- Watch technique video

Figure 48-1. Ankle or knee (lower extremity) injury workout

If the athlete's elbow, arm, or shoulder is injured, have him perform these lower-body exercises and drills:

- Butterfly, groin stretch, and toe touch flexibility exercises
- Eight sets of duck walks across the field or gym
- 10 sets of shuffling, carioca, and/or hopping across the field or gym
- 100 sit-ups
- 20 to 30 minutes of running laps (jogging, sprints, fast walk)
- 20 minutes of stance/position practice
- 10 minutes of step-ups on bleacher steps
- Barbell squats (little or no weight on the bar)
- Six sets on a hack squat machine
- Plyometrics
- Personal technique instruction
- Watch technique video

Figure 48-2. Elbow, arm, or shoulder injury workout

#49: Repair Breakdowns

What about those athletes who never seem to fulfill their potential or always want to quit? You may hear from them, "I can't win. He's [the opponent] too good." This type of athlete is often an erratic performer who looks like a champion one day and a chump the next. For him, the underlying problem often is an intense fear of not measuring up, of not performing successfully in the next competition. It may be that he dreads being successful, although he is aware that his teammates and coaches are ready to congratulate him for any achievement. His motivation is broken and needs repair.

A variety of factors can be involved, some of which you may not be able to alter. However, you can deal effectively with the athlete troubled by the mental or physical strains of the sport and wanting to quit. Often, quitting occurs when the athlete is struggling with failure. A knowledgeable and caring coach should recall a positive moment and review it. Don't lie to him or give false praise, but certainly point out improvement.

In regards to the physical demands of the sport that may be overwhelming the athlete, the coach needs to explain that the athlete isn't alone. All athletes, even the great ones, hate the physical punishment required when preparing to compete.

Sometimes athletes want to quit because the satisfaction and reward of wearing the uniform is overshadowed by the realization that they are obligated to work harder than they ever have before. These athletes need to understand that hard work produces success, but not necessarily victories.

Other typical breakdowns can be poor relations with teammates and communication problems with the coach, among others. Some of the more common reasons for quitting are highlighted here. Quitting often is not an individual decision made by the athlete. Others—family, friends, teachers—may have influenced it, but overall, athletes choose to quit when:

- Their peers tell them to
- They resent their teammates
- They resent or distrust the coach
- Alcohol or drugs have become more important
- The sport is no longer enjoyable (burn out)
- Family problems interfere
- They fear injury or the physical grind
- Academic problems surface

Many athletes decide to quit to relieve the burden of confronting their own inadequacies. So what can you do? Initially, you should try to talk out the problem. Sometimes, the athlete has set such a difficult goal that the challenge to accomplish it has overwhelmed him. You can help set a more realistic goal and encourage persistence to reach it. The root cause will always relate to at least one of his intrinsic motivational needs that is not being satisfied.

If it is failure that is interfering, model how to cope with failure and emphasize skill improvement rather than winning. Clarify and highlight those moments when the athlete has been successful and allow him to "savor" those achievements. And definitely involve the parents. Invite them and any other athletes to talk to the athlete. Above all, keep a positive, patient attitude. One junior varsity football player is even more succinct: "A motivational coach won't let you quit, even if you aren't good at the sport."

#50: Be Flexible

You must recognize that some athletes shuffle passively toward competitions while others strut with overconfidence, and it can be a struggle to motivate athletes who lack commitment to you, the program, or their teammates. However, if you identify and promote their intrinsic needs they can be productive members of your program and achieve their individual potential. You must be willing to be flexible—for example, giving the squad a heated pep talk one day and simply patting one kid's back the next.

When you begin to coach, you will probably discover at least one athlete who wants to be on the team but doesn't want to be coached. He may like to compete, even enjoy working hard at practice, but he doesn't want any input from you. He is, in short, "uncoachable."

Frequently, coaches define "coachability" in terms of how well the athlete follows directions or acquires the skills they teach. A coach may expect coachable athletes to have a good rapport with him, to respect his decisions, and to involve him if they have personal problems. When problems do occur, coaches who are not flexible sometimes doubt the athlete's willingness to be coached. Many signs of athletes being uncoachable may surface, and you must ask yourself the following questions about such an athlete.

- Does he refuse to train with the rest of the team?

- Does he sulk, whine, or complain when things don't go his way?

- Does he behave in a belligerent way or get in fights with teammates?

- Does he often fail to try his best at practice or in competitions?

- Does he "showboat" during competitions or berate opponents?

- Does he refuse to adhere to any training schedule or fail to be punctual at meetings or practice?

- Does he demonstrate disrespect for you or constantly test your authority?

This type of athlete may continually avoid you or make excessive demands (for example, for special equipment or extra time). The uncoachable athlete may find fault with the way you manage the team and disrupt practice to argue aspects of technique or strategy. Instructions may have to be repeated, equipment or uniforms may have to replaced, and confrontations with teammates may have to be arbitrated. Suddenly it is not one athlete's motivation that you must deal with, but with the motivation of every team member.

Such disruptive behaviors make everyone uncomfortable and tense. Dr. Bruce C. Ogilvie, Ph.D., and Dr. Thomas A. Tutko, Ph.D., researched athletes like this and published their results in *Problem Athletes and How to Handle Them*. They concluded that coachability is one of the most essential characteristics for superior athletic performances.

When confronted with an uncoachable athlete, a common first reaction is simple: Get rid of him. But if you see the potential for change, then a method exists for dealing with this type of individual. The key point is to determine the athlete's level of trust. Maybe he has been exploited before and now finds it difficult to have any kind of an effective rapport with a coach.

Ironically, when the flexible coach approaches the uncoachable athlete in a sincere attempt to communicate, the dialogue often backfires. For the coach, the conversation means advice and compassion. To the athlete, it's criticism. What, then, should you do? Ogilivie and Tutko offer some guidelines:

- Be reliable by saying what you will do and doing what you say.
- React positively when athletes offer reasonable suggestions for change.
- Be careful about scheduling workouts—put them in writing and post them in the locker room. Then be punctual with your own attention to these activities.
- Give athletes options.
- Don't make promises you can't keep.
- Avoid being judgmental; show tolerance for their inadequacies.
- Don't overemphasize their failures, especially as a means to change their inappropriate behavior.
- Don't get into power struggles (or be manipulated).
- Remind the athlete of your position as coach; your obligation above anything else is to the team as a whole.
- Negate any hostility with a calm and disarming demeanor.
- Don't give the uncoachable athlete responsibility as a means of changing his behavior (like making him a team captain).
- Don't lose patience.
- Be cautious when using criticism.
- Don't let their actions negate your ability to coach the rest of the team.
- Don't be afraid to dismiss an athlete from the team, regardless of his talent or potential.

It takes time, effort, and flexibility to deal with a difficult athlete and it may or may not turn out as time well spent. A veteran coach who has had winning teams at three different schools is always willing to work with this kind of athlete. "A coach has to remember," he says, "how high school really was. A coach must always be ready to communicate and be flexible. Patience is also important. Sometimes you have to sacrifice personal time or adjust your priorities on what is really important."

In their research, Ogilvie and Tutko discovered that this type of athlete often operates under a feeling of fear. The wise coach, therefore, should "develop a subtle technique for talking about fear and its effects upon performance . . . Coaches who expose their own personal fears as experiences in athletics pave the most sensitive roads to dealing with this emotion." This fear often surfaces in athletes who are experiencing some type of pressure or stress.

Potential conflicts with an athlete are lessened when you get clear information about his specific goals, either through conversation or via his first meeting questionnaire. To then change behavior, discover why he's behaving that way. Show sympathy and tolerance, but not resignation. Then present options that are both nonthreatening and different (they can't be the same ones he has heard from parents or teachers). Decide together and follow through until the athlete realizes he can gain more from ending the conflict than from continuing it. The ultimate goal should be to motivate this athlete, not dismiss him.

#51: Prompt Physical Preparation

Young athletes have to be told that getting in shape means experiencing various levels of discomfort. No one likes to work to exhaustion, but being an athlete does require daily doses of fatigue. You probably have discovered that working athletes too hard in practice discourages some kids, but working them too lightly leaves them physically unprepared for competitions. Your players can find practice to be an enjoyable, motivational, and enriching experience, regardless of its difficulty, if you:

- Occasionally let team leaders run practice
- Can list examples of matches where their physical conditioning has resulted in victory
- Can point out how tapping into physical reservoirs of energy produces power
- Have them pretend that, "Today is the last practice of the season. Make it your best!"
- Use a variety of drills
- Know when to push and when to call it a day

Consider Carl Lewis, who was one of the best track athletes of all time. When an interviewer asked Tom Tellez, his coach, to summarize the factors that prompted Lewis' phenomenal success, he said, "I attribute his success to his parents, his home life, and his stability . . . I don't like to overwork kids . . . I work on mechanics. You prepare the athlete mentally by preparing him physically."

A high school football player says, "I love competition, and I want to stay in shape. That's what motivates me. During the summer I set a goal to get in 200 hours of work. I got in 241 hours. My coach helped a lot. He always has a positive attitude—he's very optimistic, very motivational."

Preparing for any competition is seldom fun for athletes because it normally involves extensive physical and mental effort, so it important that you acknowledge that fact and be ready to recognize those athletes who maintain a positive outlook through the grind of practice. Point out their efforts and praise them when they are successful at practice to build their confidence and increase their motivation.

#52: Use the Media

To be sure, working with the media takes persistence, because too often the local newspapers, radio, and television stations are more interested in professional teams, but you should send them media releases anyway and invite them to do brief profiles on the team as a whole or on some outstanding athletes. Almost all college, high school, and middle school players are motivated when they see this coverage.

Provide this information to the media in a news-style format and encourage them to attend the next match or tournament. Keep sending the media releases (Figure 52-1) regardless of whether the information is published. Contact local news sources by telephone and try to make a friend at each location. If you can get one reporter or broadcaster on your side, his assistance can do wonders for your program.

High School Media Release

To: _____ **Date:** _____

From: Head Coach

Re: Richmond Heights Invitational Wrestling Tournament Placers

The Richmond Heights High School Spartans won the team championship trophy at their own invitational tournament ahead of a field of 16 teams on Saturday, _____ .

The following athletes achieved placement:

Brian Smith (103)	Champion
Bill Smith (119)	Runner-up
Matt Musarra (125)	Runner-up
Mike Connely (135)	Fourth Place
Herb Adkins (140)	Champion
Pat Campolieti (145)	Champion
Joe Daugherty (152)	Third Place
Greg Leinweber (171)	Champion
Dan Agresta (HWT)	Fourth Place

The Spartan's current dual meet record is 5-1 and they compete next in a quad match at Norwalk High School on _____ (date).

For further information call _____ .

Any time between _____ and _____ .

Figure 52-1. Media release

Work to get the athletes' names and accomplishments in the newspaper or on the radio and inform them (and their parents) when it happens. Invite the media to interview you and/or your better players. Then send a thank you note to the media for their coverage. You should also invite media personnel to your awards program at the end of the season and write a thank you letter for the publicity they provided during the season (Figure 52-2).

Dear _____

Your coverage of our game against _____ High School effectively described the competitive effort put forth by both teams. It was an exciting match, and all the athletes, coaches, and parents associated with our program are grateful you reported on it.

We are especially pleased that you highlighted several individual performances. Overall, your article was informative and entertaining. Our parents, students, and staff look forward to reading more like it.

Again, thanks for the recent article and your continued coverage _____ of wrestling.

With appreciation,

Figure 52-2. Thank you letter to the media

#53: Use the Public Address System

Each week during the season you must use your school's public address system to highlight and acknowledge the accomplishments of your team and individual players (Figure 53-1). You bring the athletes both recognition in front of their peers and a sense of pride for their participation on the team. Hearing their names and then receiving compliments from classmates is very motivational to young athletes. Be sure you do this on a regular basis and vary the names of your players as much as possible.

A special congratulations to the varsity girls tennis team! Number one singles Jenny Jones won her tenth match of the season, and the doubles team of Margaret Mitchell and Christine Smith defeated their opponents 6-0, 6-1. The Mitchell-Smith combination is undefeated for the season. Also winning their matches were Sarah Brett and Emily Lee.

The varsity girls tennis team in next in action on Thursday at 4:00 PM in DeSan Park. You should check out the best team in the league.

Figure 53-1. Public address announcement

#54: Give Pep Talks

When many coaches envision a pregame locker room pep talk, they see Knute Rockne's "Win this one for the Gipper" speech. Such drama doesn't motivate all athletes and many times it isn't even needed. In fact, such a speech might even be counterproductive.

Pep talks need not be emotional tirades. More often, they should be business-like in tone and format. You should express as clearly and as briefly as possible what awaits the athletes and what is expected of them. Whether you want to provoke your athletes or not, you should be straightforward and honest. You must demonstrate calmness and confidence, especially when the athletes seem tense or uncertain, and use emotion only if the timing seems right.

Adhere to the following five guidelines when using a pep talk to motivate athletes:

- *Have a theme.* Expressing a specific, straightforward message is important. It could be about perseverance, poise, or points. You decide the subject, select the words, give an illustration to help them understand, and be sure they're attentive.

- *Eliminate distractions.* In the locker room, don't give the pep talk when they're dressing, listening to music, or adjusting their uniform or equipment. Athletes should be seated, relaxed, and quiet.

- *Avoid gimmicks and impromptu pep talks.* Most of these are doomed to fail. And don't make promises (like to shave your head or run behind the bus), since such stunts lead more to amusement than motivation.

- *Allow others to give the pep talk.* No rule says the coach must be the one to always give the pep talk. Community leaders, former athletes, popular teachers, or administrators can speak to the team before a competition or at practices. Even better, athletes can give each other pep talks if you guide them correctly through that process.

- *Determine the best intensity level of the pep talk.* Getting athletes "psyched up" has its rewards and its faults. One athlete may need a high level of energy while another performs better when the motivation is more low-key. Each athlete's energy level needs to be evaluated; personality, attitude, and maturity need to be assessed. If the athlete is introverted, less psyching is recommended, but not so low that he remains indifferent toward the competition.

For complex tasks, or if many competitions await the athlete (as in a tournament), then less psyching up is usually needed. Furthermore, a more experienced athlete often needs less of a pep talk.

Pep talks are a part of all sports, and most athletes can often still recall many years later their coaches' comments, good or bad, before an important competition. That said, the wise coach considers carefully much in advance the pep talk he wants to give before a game or tournament and then speaks to the team in such a manner that the athletes compete with inspiration.

#55: Videotape Your Athletes

Videotape can serve as a great way to teach and motivate athletes. Many methods are available to give feedback to athletes when evaluating their performances, but a favorite of many athletes is videotape. Videotape the athletes' performance and then view the tape later to analyze their strong and weak points. Your positive commentary can add to their motivation.

Young athletes love watching themselves on television. Whether their performances were below or above expectations, they simply enjoy seeing themselves in action. You should exploit this and videotape them as much as possible—at selected practices, weekly competitions, the team party, etc. Then let them view the tape as soon as possible after the event so they can get immediate feedback. You may decide to make a highlight tape for the team or even each player with graphics and music dubbed in to show at your awards program or a final team banquet. Using this technology can do much to motivate today's athlete.

#56: Show Videos

You can purchase videotapes of outstanding college and professional athletes or teams in almost every sport. These highlight films are professionally produced and very motivational. Your athletes can observe talented college and professional athletes in action, possibly hear commentary from them and their coaches, and enjoy a background soundtrack of popular music and professional announcers. You could also use these videos to talk about the great athletes who were highly committed. As you show videotapes of these individuals, comment on their intensity, enthusiasm, and perseverance. These videos can both teach and inspire young athletes, and every coach should employ them at least once or twice during the season.

#57: Mail a Newsletter

Newsletters are invaluable. They are the most effective way for any sports program or school group to advertise its achievements and communicate to its athletes and fans. By profiling the team and your athletes' individual accomplishments, a newsletter can be a powerful tool for low-cost public relations. A newsletter promotes your program and generates motivation.

The parents, local media, school administrators, and fellow teachers all deserve to be informed about the team's progress throughout the season (throughout the year in some cases). Newsletters update parents, fans, the administration, and the community on individual and team results, new rules, and upcoming events, increasing their interest in the program and building your credibility and professional standing. Reading about themselves and the team keeps athletes motivated because you have presented them in a positive manner. You could also use a newsletter to convey special motivational messages.

No matter what type of newsletter you eventually design, you are conveying an important image to your athletes and the community (especially parents). Formats and styles of newsletters can vary, but all should provide some common information:

- An introduction that grabs the readers' attention on the first page and keeps them reading:

  Have our hearts recovered? Those nail-biting victories over Aurora and Newbury certainly caused the adrenaline to flow and the cheers to erupt. My kids . . . Your kids . . . Our kids were psyched and relentless. They demanded the victory and they got it! To be sure, your presence and support really helped make it happen.

- Game and tournament results

- Dates and times of upcoming competitions

- Updates or announcements about important events or honors that involve the team or individual athletes

  The team finished as United Press International's number one rated school in Division III for the season, which was determined by the votes of coaches across the state.

  Tickets for the state basketball tournament are $25.00/packet and can be purchased from the athletic director.

- Individual statistics

- Comments from assistant coaches and/or administrators

"I'm enjoying the opportunity to coach these young student-athletes, but I caution them to be 'doers' and not 'talkers.' We can not relax. Instead, we must continue to strive toward becoming the best we can be." – Assistant Coach

- Inspirational quotes

  "Courage is not how a man stands or falls, but how he gets back up again." – John L. Lewis

- A trivia question

  What athlete holds the record for most career tennis wins at our school?

- Reminders related to dates and times of special events or the collection of equipment and uniforms

- Public thank you notes to administrators and/or parents

  Thanks to Mrs. Patricia Raiff, our principal, and Dr. Marc Crail, superintendent, for the dedicated support of our program. They remained constantly attentive to the needs of the coaching staff and showed a special understanding of our athletes. We owe our success in part to you.

You could also use the newsletter to post an Athlete of the Week award winner, the players' academic honors, or your athletes' accomplishments in other sports. You should also list the significant details related to your program—tournament results, team picnic, fund-raisers, rules clarifications.

Maybe one of your more artistic athletes can assist you in creating a unique and bold logo or masthead for your newsletter. You can also use colorful graphics, high-quality illustrations, and vivid photographs. Be sure the print is clear and easy to read.

If you can establish a positive connection between yourself and the parents, your position in the school and community becomes more prominent and your team itself becomes more popular and motivated. As always, effective communication is the key. A newsletter can accomplish this for you.

#58: Utilize Community Organizations

Too many coaches neglect school and community organizations who themselves are seeking ways to get involved in the school and help—and motivate—students. These groups of adults can support your program and serve indirectly to motivate athletes. The first step is to contact them and seek their support.

Potential support groups in the community are the Booster Club, Kiwanis, Rotary, American Legion, Lions, Chamber of Commerce, and local churches. By obtaining the support of these clubs, your program may enjoy the financial and political support that most successful programs need to prosper. Begin by writing a letter to each organization's president to introduce yourself and your program—a brief history and current expectations. Explain in your letter how you may want them to contribute to the team—attending matches, making a donation, hosting a special event (an all-star wrestling match, for example), or purchasing some supplies. You should also request the opportunity to speak at their next meeting. A brief, enthusiastic speech can not only acquaint them with the team, but also intensify their interest in your program. Maintain a connection and update them by sending them your media guide, newsletter, and schedule and returning to their meetings to speak.

Don't neglect your own school board. Go to their meetings to announce updates about the team and to acknowledge specific players publicly. Later, have your players write thank you letters to specific individuals on any organization that supports your program (Figure 58-1).

This connection to the community can do much for you, your program, and your players. When they know they have the total support of adults outside their families, most athletes are both appreciative and inspired.

Dear Mr. _____ :

The _____ High School _____ team is indeed grateful to you for your support of our program. Your generous donation of much-needed funds enabled us to purchase Gatorade for use during our tournaments and after our games.

The coaches and players truly appreciate your interest and generosity. It is wonderful to recognize that there are community members like yourself interested in seeing our program succeed. We will certainly commit ourselves to fulfilling the expectations the community has for our program.

Once again, thank you for your dedicated effort directed toward our program. It is exciting to see community members support our players so enthusiastically. We hope to see you attend one or all of our competitions so we can thank you personally (a schedule is enclosed).

Gratefully,

The Coaching Staff and Players of _____ High School

Figure 58-1. Thank you letter to a community member

#59: Provide Awards

One varsity track athlete identifies his focus as an athlete: "I enjoy playing sports with my friends, but I participate for the awards of trophies and medals." A college wrestler adds: "Right now I'm only into it to qualify for Nationals." Sports psychologist Dr. Robert Weinberg surveyed junior and senior high school athletes and discovered many were motivated by the extrinsic rewards.

Awards can do much to satisfy most athletes' desire for a tangible reward for their efforts. These weekly or monthly awards can be plaques, trophies, medals, certificates, T-shirts, ribbons, or patches for letter jackets, accompanied of course by a public address announcement the next day.

You may choose to give awards for the top performance at practice each week, for the top performance (though not necessarily a victorious one) at the most recent competition, or for a display of outstanding sportsmanship or community service. Whatever your award or the criteria attached to it, awards can do much to motivate many players.

#60: Acknowledge Contributions

Make sure that each athlete knows he is making a strong contribution to the program. To keep athletes motivated, you have to make them feel special to the team. Their personal achievements have to be recognized and praised. They have to know that you care about them personally and that they are making an important contribution to helping the team achieve its goals. It's also okay to brag about their accomplishments in the school and in the community.

Second, positive praise is important, especially for the athletes who are junior varsity. They are as important to any program as the superstars and should be treated with as much attention as the varsity. In the case of marginal athletes, well-phrased compliments enhance their sense of belonging and self-esteem.

#61: Stick Signs in Their Yards

In Chillicothe, Illinois, the mothers construct and paint signs to put in the front yards of each football player—ninth through twelfth grade. Since the school (Illinois Valley Central High School) nickname is "Grey Ghosts," they print in crimson letters "Home of a Grey Ghost FB Player" with the grey outline of a ghost behind it on a three-foot square sign. This type of motivation can work in any town and community. Moreover, a sign adds to a player's sense of team pride and recognition. It invites compliments, offers of good luck, and congratulations after competitions. Coaches, art students, student council members, parents, and pep clubs can all contribute to the design, construction, and distribution of these signs, which can go a long way toward motivating athletes.

#62: Decorate their Lockers

In many schools the cheerleaders decorate the lockers of every athlete during their season of competition. They tape to the locker the player's number, school logo, picture, and good luck signs, along with colored crepe paper and possibly balloons. Over the course of the season, decorations related to that week's upcoming contest (e.g., "Beat the Panthers!") are added. This brings each athlete team recognition, personal satisfaction, and individual motivation.

Decorating lockers can do much to motivate athletes, but be sure school that administrators, custodians, and teachers are informed about your intentions. If the cheerleaders are too busy, you can ask the student council, pep club, art club, or team managers to do this for the players.

#63: Describe Success

Some athletes just want to be members of the team. Since they care little about success, they don't want to be responsible for winning or losing. In this way, these underachievers can avoid blame or criticism. An important duty for a coach, then, is to prepare athletes to triumph, especially those kids who only have infrequent experiences with success. All coaches need to define and describe success for athletes to motivate them to pursue both team and individual success.

Start with yourself first. A winning coach sets high standards and succeeds because he expects to succeed. When a negative belief enters his mind ("We just can't run the ball against anyone"), he quickly replaces it with a positive one ("Okay then, we're going to be the best passing team in the conference"). This approach may seem Pollyannaish, but it is a common mindset of successful people. On a practical level, this outlook requires you to:

- Analyze your situation (e.g., the team has difficulty running the football)
- Design an advantage (e.g., we'll work harder on passing the ball)
- Believe enthusiastically that the plan will succeed and set a goal (e.g., we'll total more passing yardage than our opponents in every conference game)

Furthermore, describe success clearly and concisely to the entire coaching staff and then the team. Answer a basic question for them: What determines a successful athlete in your sport? For example, what makes up a successful high school golfer? Or a winning football team? Or a champion gymnast?

Defining success and discussing strategy with your players for a few minutes each day affirms their acceptance of those standards and enhances their motivation. Relate to them how their practice activities help lead to success, for example as a golfer, a football team, or a gymnast. Completing these activities in practice with enthusiasm and diligence must become everyone's priority. Repetition of these affirmations leads to mastery. It also keeps your players focused.

You can even help your players visualize success. For example, a football coach took his team in full uniform during the first week of practice to the stadium where the state championship game would be held 18 weeks later and put them through their pregame warm-up as if they were to play the game that day. A wrestling coach made his wrestlers stand on a victory podium and played a tape of recorded cheering as if they have just won a tournament. A golf coach showed a videotape of professional golfers, one after another, sinking amazing putts. A baseball coach had season tickets to the Cleveland Indians and takes two of three players to each game and comments on the skills of the players on the field. The intent of each of these coaches is simple: Here is what success feels like and looks like; let's make it happen for us.

Most coaches already have the basic characteristics of a winning, competitive personality. They know how to present themselves as motivated and positive individuals. When you respond to your athletes in these ways, you get better results from them in practice and competition.

But you must do more to help athletes accept your definition of success. You need to have faith that they can be successful and keep repeating your description of success. The following are quotes from high school athletes on this subject:

- "The coach has to believe in me and give me a chance."

- "My performance improved because my coach had faith in me."

- "My coach kept pushing me to greater achievements and setting even higher goals."

- "They were my role models, and they made me strive to be my best."

- "Our strength and conditioning coach made the greatest difference for me. [He] made me run and lift weights when I didn't want to. At times I thought he was a jerk. Now, I have the utmost respect for this man. I can honestly say I owe all my success to him."

#64: Expect Positive Outcomes

Expecting positive outcomes means you have confidence, and when you demonstrate confidence in yourself and your athletes, you discover the power of charisma. You don't have to be movie-star charming, but you do have to be direct and committed to expecting positive outcomes.

You can capitalize on players' intrinsic motivation by challenging them to learn new techniques and predicting with enthusiasm that they will master them. If they fail to master them right away, show no concern or worry. In fact, tolerate those mistakes as natural to any learning process, especially if you expect a positive outcome. Work, then, to eliminate errors through drill sessions, instruction, and positive reinforcement. A junior high soccer player appreciates his coaches because, "They don't let you quit when they know you can do it."

To be sure, the biggest obstacle to positive outcomes is criticism and confrontations. No athlete or coach escapes some form of disapproval during his career. Yet, with effort, every coach can transform this negative energy into a positive, productive outcome by doing the following:

- Anticipate problems before they reach the crisis stage
- Maintain a professional demeanor even when others are dominated by their emotions
- Remain assertive but not confrontational when dealing with opposing points of view
- Repair damaged relationships through compromise and cooperation
- Recognize the differences between healthy and harmful anger in the players and show them how to channel this emotion into effort, not antagonism
- Confront difficult people and situations directly without being intimidated or provoked
- Be regularly accessible for others when a problem comes up
- Communicate in an honest, straightforward way with athletes
- Establish yourself as a person to be trusted and respected
- Refuse to let any kind of criticism ruin your effectiveness as a coach

#65: Be Attentive

"The coach we hire must have a solid value system that places importance on kindness to others and on hard work to achieve quality," says middle school principal Hans Pesch. "The individual must show genuine care for athletes and know how to teach that attitude to them." Pesch's statement emphasizes the importance of coaches showing concern for their athletes' welfare and being attentive to their personal needs. A high school baseball player adds: "It's important that the coach is more than a coach. He's a friend, too. He has to understand me and discipline me."

Being attentive also means giving feedback when necessary. This could occur through a private or team discussion about progress, a critique of technique, or praise for a strong effort. You could give your players weekly, possibly daily, notification of their development through posted charts or statistics.

You should also provide specific information about performances (practice or competition) to the players who have set their own training goals. This constant assessment—which must be constructive and specific to each athlete—encourages athletes to set personal standards for their practice and, hence, their matches. Good, specific compliments include statements like, "You never stopped hustling during practice today. You're setting a standard I'd like everyone to follow. Well done!" or "Your finish on your single leg was excellent. Do it that way all the time and no one will stop it." In fact, athletes should be given some indication of their improvement after each practice. That shows you are being attentive.

Sometimes, subordinates may feel uncertain about approaching you with their ideas or concerns. Don't be so wrapped up in your own agenda that you tune out. Also, never ignore your athletes, which suggests that you are apathetic and uncaring. This type of behavior lowers their morale and decreases their motivation. Instead, present opportunities for dialogue with your athletes as often as possible and always listen attentively. Simply listening with true interest and responding positively can do much to motivate young athletes.

#66: Be a Counselor

This may be a duty you would rather not accept, but to motivate today's athletes you should always be ready to counsel them about their personal problems. This is crucial because so many young athletes do not have a positive home life. "I get motivated when I know the coach is concerned about every athlete on the team from the best to the worst," says one high school football player. "A coach has to be like a second father who can teach you about sports and life."

Being a counselor can simply mean maintaining regular dialogues with players in situations other than practice that don't include nagging them about their school work or their last competition. Build motivation by recognizing when an athlete's personal problems are affecting performance and assist him in eliminating those problems.

Once coaches accept this responsibility, they are more likely to increase the motivation level of their athletes. The players and general public will come to admire them for their commitment and sincerity, their compassion and concern. Coaches who also act as counselors will probably enjoy a loyal following as well.

#67: Reduce Anxiety

How much does success depend on the athlete's physical skills and how much is in his mental attitude to the sport? If you consider the players' psychological approach, you are probably addressing their frustrations, worries, and self-esteem. To lessen athletes' anxieties, how much of a psychologist does a coach have to be?

You don't have to be Sigmund Freud. You do, however, have to be prepared to identify the emotional and psychological state of your players, especially in the ways they react to success and failure.

For some people, achievement is accompanied by anxiety. As a winning coach, you may face the pressure of staying successful, repeating a championship, or setting new standards of excellence. Though victory can be exhilarating, success can present a fresh set of problems.

It is the same for your athletes, who may feel pressure to recreate the achievement and win the "big" game each and every time, even if it is at the state tournament. Fans and parents may expect these accomplishments every season. Some athletes then find themselves struggling not to lose rather than striving to win.

It is this stress that can weaken a player's effectiveness. During every week of a typical season, athletes can experience tension caused by conflicts with teammates and/or parents. Even their own competitive attitude can lead to anxiety as they push themselves to win games. In this kind of domain, disagreements are common and confrontations are frequent. If they are not handled effectively, it is possible that the player's composure can collapse and his motivation suffer.

Many potentially successful performances are lost just prior to game-time due to getting "psyched out," losing confidence, becoming unfocused, or experiencing something unexpected. You must prepare your athletes to cope with all potentially debilitating events.

What are the stress situations that can get in the way of success? Typical stress-inducing situations include personal frustrations in school, arguments with family or friends, previous failures at a competition, and unfamiliar settings (e.g., 5,000 fans at the district tournament vs. 200 at a home game).

Look first for symptoms associated with anxiety, which include doubt, anger, frustration, negativity, regrets, and even poor health. Athletes may leave conflicts unresolved and sometimes overreact to challenges. They may complain of stomach cramps and loss of appetite, lose concentration, withdraw from others, talk too often about the season being over, or overreact to minor problems. If they can eliminate their own self-destructive behaviors and emotional surges, they can become better athletes.

Some athletes, when confronting stress, choose to avoid it by quitting. Some sports psychologists call this "burnout." Alternate terminology includes "mental fatigue" and "getting stressed out."

What is it, therefore, that you can do to turn worry into winning and tension into triumph? You may need some lessons on the psychology of pressure and the power of positive thinking to keep your athletes motivated.

Feeling pressure is, in effect, a complaint about a problem. Whether the goal is to master a baton handoff for a relay or sink two foul shots, an athlete may feel there's *something* wrong and so he cannot succeed. Suddenly, more than one obstacle exists: the actual problem and the anxiety.

Most individuals try to hide their anxiety, but this can exacerbate the problem. Although unpleasant, all this worry must be talked about and brought out into the open. The pressure, even the feeling of fear, has to be acknowledged. The stress can't be ignored or belittled.

Understanding pressure means dealing with anxiety, especially the anxiety of an uncertain outcome. For too many athletes, their imaginations often dramatize failure rather than success. Their opponents become stronger than they really are and their own weaknesses are magnified.

Stress cannot be overcome with emotion. Disgust, anger, and rage do nothing to improve skills or smarts. Therefore, it is important for you to explain that every competition involves uncertainty. This shouldn't be feared. It should be enjoyed. Winning in sports is especially exciting when it occurs against an opponent who possesses equal or greater ability. Athletes and coaches should exert faith in their abilities, not fury. Roy Campanella achieved great success as a major league baseball player and coach. He later confronted his paralysis with the same dynamic attitude. He gives excellent advice: "When you're in a slump, you don't feel sorry for yourself. That's when you have to try harder. You have to have faith, hope, and conviction that you can lick it . . . You just have to be mentally tough."

Often, an essential element to mental preparation is to remove the tension associated with taking a risk. For example, you can create problem scenarios in practice—"We're losing by one goal, we have the puck by our net, and there are only 30 seconds to go in the final period. What should we do?"—and invite his players to solve them, encouraging them to be unafraid to take the risk that could result in victory.

Utilize the following 10 techniques with your athletes to help them defeat anxiety and stay motivated:

- Direct them to a coach, fellow athlete, family member, clergyman, or teacher to help talk out the problem.

- Establish a means of relaxation that includes some form of meditation, deep breaths, and a warm-up that leaves them relaxed and alert.

- Explain instructions carefully, especially before a game. This eliminates any uncertainties about what is expected or demanded.

- Make your players familiar with what may be unfamiliar to them (e.g., play loud music in practice to simulate crowd noise).

- Demand that they always stay under control and concentrate during a competition.

- Remind them about what they should and should not eat (nutrition).

- Be sure they are knowledgeable about any information associated with a particular competition (for example, if it is a double-elimination or single-elimination tournament).

- Discuss their expectations and share your own' expectations.

- Demand that they listen to coaches, captains, and officials.

- Keep reminding them that they are strong, worthy competitors who can succeed.

In truth, virtually all athletes perceive competitions as threatening because a possibility of defeat is always present. It is the unexpected that prompts stress to occur for most athletes.

Dr. Martin Stein, a professor of pediatrics at the University of California-San Diego School of Medicine, clarifies that "the experience of tension or stress is a normal aspect of development. It's a part of every child's life, from infancy to adolescence." Coaches shouldn't feel hesitant about "taking the first steps to discuss a problem with school staff—nurses, teachers, counselors, or support workers—and the child's family." Stein offers two more strategies: teach in creative ways and be ready to communicate. Have athletes concentrate on tasks, not outcomes.

A successful coach/athlete relationship requires a balance of respect, confidence, and comfort. Coaches must create an atmosphere that lessens the athletes' stress and allows them to feel a sense of control. Any sports season is a journey, sometimes a long one, for athletes who undoubtedly will encounter obstacles and difficulties. You, therefore, must be prepared for this.

#68: Counteract Peer Pressure

Another type of stress that can hinder motivation is the pressure athletes receive from their peers. They may be pressured to break training rules, skip practice, participate in underage drinking, or use illegal drugs. Satisfying the needs of friends is a strong motivator for most young people, and today's coaches must work hard to prevent their athletes from becoming victims of peer pressure, which preys upon their moods and emotions. Your athletes can better deal with peer pressure if you prepare them ahead of time to both recognize and resist it.

Keep in mind that you cannot pick the athletes' friends for them, and you cannot order them to abandon certain friends regardless of your worries about their backgrounds or intentions. Approach them instead with questions: How do your friends support you as an athlete? What are they doing to help you succeed? How often do they attend your competitions? Do they encourage or discourage you from breaking training rules? What are their attitudes toward this team and the coaches?

Avoid lecturing. They may tune you out or, worse, challenge your authority. The goal is to help athletes make the right decision when faced with peer pressure. Posing questions and possibly offering some personal anecdotes about when you confronted peer pressure are strong ways to get athletes thinking about the correct choice to make.

You might also role play some scenarios that involve peer pressure, creating a game of "What would you do if . . .?" Emphasize the mental toughness they have as athletes and boost their emotional self-esteem when their responses to the role play are effective. Also, encourage teammates to support each other, and remind them that the team as "family" can help everyone deal with any type of peer pressure.

When you show your athletes through questions and anecdotes that you understand peer pressure and then express faith that they can deal with it successfully on their own, you increase their personal levels of confidence in both you and themselves. When you as the coach remind your players to take pride and pleasure in their athletic achievements and clarify their strong points as athletes, you assist them in overcoming peer pressure from outside your program. And finally, when you model ways to react to peer pressure, you prepare them ahead of time to handle it. The unfortunate reality is that most kids will confront peer pressure almost daily, so the wise coach must be ready to deal with it frequently to keep athletes motivated.

#69: Take Pictures

If it is true that a picture is worth a thousand words, then it makes sense that pictures can motivate athletes. Either have a professional or amateur photographer—possibly a parent—take pictures of your athletes at practice, in competitions, and during any training session, and then post them in display cases and in classrooms. You may even place them on the windows or doors of community businesses. Be sure captions accompany the pictures identifying the athletes' names and the situation (e.g., Jenny Jones and Sally Smith leap for a rebound against Bay High School).

Arrange for the school newspaper and yearbook to publish pictures of your players. With today's digital cameras this is easily accomplished. You can request that managers, statisticians, or the spirit club complete a scrapbook for each senior athlete who then receives it at the awards program at the end of the season.

You can also take pictures of your Player of the Week, at both the varsity and junior varsity levels, and post them in a display case or on a locker room bulletin board. Update these as often as possible because photographs can have a strong influence on your players' motivation.

#70: Be Encouraging

For most athletes, encouragement must be continuous and constructive. Athletes feel encouraged when they realize you are dedicated to their personal success and find multiple opportunities to commend their actions and achievements.

Remember, achievement can have nothing to do with wins. It can have no relationship at all to the numbers on the scoreboard. You should, in fact, never base achievement on outcomes. You probably need to define achievement in as many ways as you have athletes. A coach who uses encouragement to motivate athletes rewards effort, not success; publicizes ability, not outcomes; and sees victory as the athlete's (or the team's), not the coach's. A coach like this uses assurance, not anger, to motivate athletes.

Athletes can also encourage other athletes. The idea is to involve athletes who have found the sport to be so rewarding and enjoyable that they are eager to tell that to younger kids. As their coach, though, be sure that your older athletes say the right things. For example, "I tell them that I play football because it's fun and exciting," says a varsity running back. "But you have to be ready to push yourself."

Most coaches agree that you don't win with the techniques you know, you win with the athletes you teach. Clearly, the athlete's physical talent and personal commitment become crucial elements in both individual and team success. Therefore, coaches should spend time encouraging their athletes to work to increase their level of commitment, motivation, and ultimately team success.

#71: Persist

The persistence to continue motivating athletes must begin with the entire coaching staff. The head coach must assemble a staff in which everyone supports each other and shares the same vision for the program. Although individuals will possess different personalities, everyone must respect each other, deal cooperatively with challenges and problems, and assist the head coach in an enthusiastic manner to motivate all athletes.

As the head coach you must constantly present yourself as a leader and a role model. You should always try to improve your ability as a leader and boost your staff's enthusiasm. You must be prepared, though, to deal with tardiness, conflicts, and emotions. Overall, your style of leadership must be consistent and confident. Present an image of calm self-confidence, but avoid being "pushy." People, especially athletes, are motivated by leaders who appear strong, positive, and relaxed even during difficult situations.

The bottom line?

Maintaining that image and a high level of motivation takes persistence. This means that you keep finding ways to appeal to your athletes' intrinsic need to do their best, extrinsic need to gain rewards, and personal reasons for enjoying competition. As you do so, be attentive to the needs of all your athletes and be sure that everyone is headed in the same direction.

#72: Teach Commitment

It is reasonable to assume that the greater the commitment by the athlete, the deeper his motivation. Therefore, if you improve the athlete's commitment, you can increase his motivation. But how can you teach athletes to become more committed to the team and the program?

First, you have to recognize that each athlete begins the season with a different level of commitment, a different reason for competing, and a different relationship with the coaching staff. You must discover how committed each athlete is, define the level of commitment you feel is necessary for team success, and, consequently, work to improve each athlete's commitment. How?

Have a private conversation with the athlete to find out how committed he is. It is best to do this before the season even begins, possibly during a free period at school or over the telephone. If this is not possible, then be sure to talk to the athlete before or after practice during the first week of the season. Ask the athlete: "What are you willing to do this year to make yourself and the team successful?"

Don't get upset or dismayed if their answers aren't dynamic descriptions of the great sacrifices they plan to make. Indeed, many kids, especially younger ones, may respond with, "I don't know." You probably will be the first coach ever to ask them this. That is when you need to define commitment for them. Explain that committed athletes:

- Do not break training rules

- Are goal-oriented (both team and individual)

- Are punctual for practices, meetings, and games

- Attend all practices

- Maintain enthusiasm and intensity during practice

- Encourage their teammates

- Enjoy challenges and work hard to accomplish them

- Are dedicated and reliable

- Are coachable and cooperative

- Are responsible students in the classroom

When you discuss commitment with athletes, it is best to point out an athlete who demonstrates these characteristics. You can also offer an example of a previous player on the team who exemplified commitment and motivation. Often, the committed athlete arrives early and stays late, maintains a positive attitude especially during a crisis, and anticipates success, not failure, before competitions.

You can even use a chart on a chalk board to simplify the teaching of commitment:

1----2----3----4----5----6----7----8----9----10

Low Level Average Level High Level

The use of numbers can sometimes clarify commitment (and motivation) for kids, just as they would recognize the impact that 80 MPH has over 40 MPH in a car. Kids with low levels of motivation (1–3) typically arrive one minute before practice begins and leave one second after you've dismissed them. They may not show much aggressiveness in competitions or much emotion about success or failure.

Their lack of commitment need not be criticized. In time, they can be motivated to work toward higher levels. "An effective coach for me," says one varsity athlete, "pushes me to the limit. It's someone who is dedicated, who gives you encouragement, but also pushes you to the next level."

Identifying players with average levels of commitment (4–7) can be frustrating for a coach. Often, these athletes are uncertain whether they should do more or less. They give medium effort at practice and have average success at competitions. They always listen to the coach at practice but may lose their focus at a crucial moment in a contest.

Once again, hold off on the criticism. Teach them first how intensifying their commitment can benefit both the team and themselves. This kind of sacrifice doesn't happen easily. You need to develop a sound relationship with each individual both on the and off the field or court. If disagreements and questions occur, it's essential that they not only respect and trust your judgments, but also know you're very interested in them as individuals.

What kind of athlete matches up to numbers 8–10? This kid practices hard and then runs at night. He is eager to learn and loves to compete. The coach may see this athlete be the first to congratulate or console a teammate after a game. This type of athlete never complains no matter what the circumstances.

Note that you cannot judge commitment by wins and losses, and commitment is truly characterized by actions, not by talk. It may be appealing to hear an athlete say, "I am committed to being a state champion" but a better statement would be, "I am committed to *practicing and competing* like a state champion."

Commitment surfaces in what the athlete is willing *to do*. A statement like "I plan to give it all I've got" does little to indicate commitment. Better statements, like the ones listed here from athletes in various sports, clarify the actions, attitude, and motivation necessary for a high level of commitment:

- "I am committed to practicing with intensity and alertness."

- "I am committed to learning all I can, following the coach's directions, and always making weight so the team doesn't have to forfeit."
- "I'm committed to practicing, learning, and acting like a state gymnastics champion."

As the season progresses, give an informal weekly progress report to each athlete during which you discuss your observations of his commitment (Figure 72-1). Review the chart if necessary: "It looks like you're operating around #6, Jenny. Let's try to get to #8 tomorrow and #10 by match day. I know you have the ability, and I have confidence in you."

You may begin by discussing effective vs. ineffective statements of commitment, and then help them verbalize their commitment in terms of what they will do, not what they want to have happen. Again, don't become discouraged if you find that the younger athletes may not be willing to do very much. Engage these athletes in making a single commitment such as increasing their total push-ups in a single practice from 50 to 100, then 150.

Finally, and most importantly, you must always demonstrate commitment in the 9–10 range. You should be the model the kids can imitate. And point out to them how the team has succeeded or improved because of their commitment. It is hoped that in time your athletes will realize the benefits of being committed.

Weekly Progress Report

Name _____ Date _____

Below is your rating in each category, which measures your level of commitment this past week (with 10 indicating a high mark and 1 indicating the lowest mark). It should be your goal to improve in each category each week.

Criteria	Rating	Coach's Comments
Dedication and determination	_____	
Mental attitude	_____	
Strength work	_____	
Physical conditioning	_____	
Cooperation with others	_____	
Competitiveness	_____	
Enthusiasm and motivation	_____	
Focus and learning	_____	
Average score	_____	

Figure 72-1. Commitment progress report

#73: Criticize Carefully

Criticism can have a damaging effect on motivation, so when critiquing athletes either formally or informally begin by having them do a self-evaluation. This precludes any defensive behavior on their part and helps maintain their motivation.

Begin by posing questions. For example: "How should we finish our single leg takedown from this position?" or "Why didn't that passing play work that time?" Then insist that your athletes give you plain, honest feedback. Admit that you don't have all the answers and be open to change. Accepting their responses as valid helps build their self-esteem and motivation.

Next, empathize with your athletes. Keep in mind that physical coordination, attention span, and experience levels vary from person to person, especially among younger athletes. Imagine yourself in their shoes before offering a criticism or complaint.

Finally, provide multiple opportunities to correct mistakes. Your athletes will probably appreciate your patience and feel less pressure to make corrections immediately. When they have made the proper corrections, praise them accordingly.

Be sure your players recognize the reasons for any criticism. Most often, a quick explanation—"Here's why it's important to do it this way"—can accomplish that. When they accept the reasons, they are more willing to take on the responsibility for correcting a mistake, for overcoming their limitations, and for reshaping their skills. The ultimate outcome is for them to take on the responsibility for their own success and/or defeat in competition.

The athletes who accept this kind of responsibility come to see instruction as an opportunity to eliminate a weakness and improve performance. After recognizing the importance of mastering a certain skill, they are eager to test themselves, even if it isn't easily accomplished. They show more effort and listen more closely. They are also more motivated.

The wise coach, therefore, prefaces instruction and criticism by first listing the reasons for correcting the error. He then provokes the athlete's sense of ambition by challenging him to persevere beyond his initial mistakes until he is convinced that the athlete's mental and physical energy is focused on mastering the maneuver and surpassing their limitations.

Put simply, coaching is teaching, and the best coaches are often the best teachers. Because criticism is often part of the learning process, be sure to provide constructive criticism and be selective in using it. If you truly care about the athlete's self-motivation and personal achievement, avoid repeating criticism and compliment their personal efforts more than you criticize their public mistakes.

#74: Show Your Mail

Showing your athletes the positive correspondence you get from college or opposing coaches can add tremendous credibility to you and your program and, in turn, provide some motivation for them to succeed on the field, court, or mat. Share with your athletes any written praise the team receives from opposing coaches (make copies if necessary), or ask team captains to read out loud letters you receive from other coaches or colleagues. Do the same for the e-mails, cards, and any direct mail you receive. You should also share complimentary correspondence from administrators, teachers, parents, and fans. Read these at the beginning of practice during announcements when the athletes are probably most attentive and eager to listen.

#75: Honor Traditions

If you are a veteran coach you probably have been honoring one tradition or another for years. Maybe it is an annual spaghetti dinner in the preseason or the distribution of a special award at the postseason awards program. Novice coaches, however, either need to adopt or create special traditions associated with their teams. Whatever your situation, establishing and honoring a team tradition can be important to the overall morale and motivation of athletes.

Traditions can certainly add credibility to any program (for example, having an alumni or hall of fame game where you honor former athletes) and can suggest a repetition of success. For example, a ceremony can be held every year for either regional or state tournament qualifiers. Many athletes are motivated to participate in programs that are seen as successful, popular sports in the school.

Be sure your traditions are not private affairs. Publicize them to all athletes, parents, school administrators, fellow coaches, community members, and support personnel. Indeed, when the entire school can participate in a tradition, team achievement and personal accomplishment are maximized. This happens because a supportive, tradition-oriented network has been established in which everyone involved in the program seeks to benefit (and motivate) someone else.

#76: Win Games

Wanting to win is never harmful. It is natural, even beneficial, to strive to win in competition. All coaches work to achieve championships for their teams and themselves. In fact, it is expected that they try to do so. Such expectations can give players purpose, direction, and motivation.

Vince Lombardi said, "It is a reality of life that men are competitive and the most competitive games draw the most competitive men. That's why they are here—to compete. The object is to win fairly, squarely, by the rules—but to win." Charlie Brown said, "Winning ain't everything, but losing is nothing."

Your challenge as a coach is to avoid attaching so much importance to wins and losses that they become the basic tenant for judging the athletic program. Often, this can debilitate your players' motivation.

According to Janet Spence, a University of Texas professor who studied 4000 employees and students, found that the most competitive people—those most interested in winning—feel the most isolated, are the most wary of others, and are the most likely to maintain a distance from their peers.

Spence's study does not suggest that coaches adopt an anticompetition attitude, but it does indicate that coaches should examine their own competitiveness before training athletes. Certainly no joy exists in losing. A loss in any form can be crushing, but in athletics rarely is it the end. Learning how to handle a setback, a hardship, or a loss prepares young people for the difficulties outside athletics and keeps them motivated.

"As teachers and coaches, we must remember that when mere winning is our only goal, we are doomed to disappointment and failure. But when our goal is to try to win, when our focus is on preparation and sacrifice and effort instead of on numbers on a scoreboard then we will never lose," says Mike Krzyzewski, Duke University basketball coach.

It is not uncommon for a coach, especially a very competitive one, to be tempted to abandon his principles because of the pressure to win. But this ultimately can work against your efforts to motivate kids and maintain employment. "We do not want a coach who wants to win at all costs," says Louis Pronga, former athletic director at Illinois Valley Central High School. "The coach should be a good role model who teaches by example. Winning is not a factor in how we hire a coach. It's more important that we get someone who has professional ethics and commitment. Sports are only one part of the educational process." Joe Paterno of Penn State recognizes that, "It is always good to know what it is to lose. I guess it means that we've got to get back to work."

Sports gives young people an opportunity to strive for excellence, to risk losing in order to learn, and to grow into successful persons. Winning should not be the end of their goal-setting; it should be only the beginning.

Furthermore, creating the circumstances that make winning happen is certainly challenging and ongoing. Each season may require new methods, but the experienced coach realizes this. Each season means you have a new team—seniors have graduated, newcomers have joined—a fresh group to teach to win. Just be careful not to sabotage your success by being overconfident or overestimating your team's strengths, or by basing achievement on any one game.

When coaches focus their program on the number of wins produced by the season's end, they are setting themselves up to ride an emotional rollercoaster. If you get too pumped up about winning and too depressed about losing, you can find yourself riding the gut-wrenching peaks and valleys of a rollercoaster track. This behavior not only can be an emotional nightmare, but it's also unhealthy.

To conclude, a high school athlete comments, "I like a coach who always pushes his team to their full potential but isn't so bent on winning that he forgets we're human."

#77: Smile (a Lot!)

It's simple: Athletes are more likely to be coachable and motivated when they see you smile, when you know all their names, and when you encourage them. Smiling means you are in a good mood, that you are content, that you are pleased with where you are and what you are doing. If kids can see that, it's easier to prompt them to want to be around you and participate in your sport.

Smiling every day, in fact, should be a top priority for successful coaching. Through every season, you may come to depend more on a friendly, outward demeanor than on any other skill or talent you have as a coach.

Because an intrinsic motivation for most young athletes is to gain approval from their peers and their coaches, they will constantly study your facial expressions and body language to determine how you are evaluating their progress. Your challenge, therefore, is to create the conditions in the practice room that capitalize on that intrinsic motivation by smiling and being friendly toward players.

You may have to work from dawn to dusk planning practices, repairing equipment, meeting with administrators, reviewing videotapes, instructing athletes and conducting drills, scouting opponents, and dialoging with parents. Such tasks can easily overwhelm even the most energetic person. But don't forget to smile!

Evaluate yourself at the end of each season by totaling your number of successful relationships, not wins and losses. Creating these kind of relationships depends on knowing first the interests and backgrounds of your athletes. Why did they join the team? In what other clubs or sports are they involved? What are their personal hobbies? To really motivate athletes, discover each one's background and show approval and acceptance for who they are and why they joined the team.

And don't forget to smile when they look at you.

#78: Be Yourself

When their teenagers take the plunge into competitive sports, parents often expect the coach to be a special surrogate parent figure who can motivate like Vince Lombardi, teach like Socrates, and win like John Wooden. Such high expectations can make even the most confident person uncertain about becoming a coach.

Do you see yourself as a Vince Lombardi or a Knute Rockne? Should you use gimmicks and theatrics to motivate your athletes? Should today's coach act more like a cheerleader? Consider these questions when deciding how you want to motivate your players. Whatever strategies you eventually employ, be sure to maintain your own identity and style when utilizing them. Gimmicks can be effective if not overdone, and finally, you need, of course, to be supportive and involved as a coach and never lose your focus during a practice or game.

A school has its mission statement. A corporation has a company policy. A coach needs his personal philosophy. You can call it your personal beliefs, professional standards, or private credo—as long as you have one. This statement should become your focus and your identity.

Just like parents who raise their children in the same manner that they were raised, coaches often adopt the coaching style of a coach who once led them. This could be a mistake if that coach's personality or style does not match your own.

Your coaching style is the summary of your personality when you enter the practice room or competition. It has little to do with what you wear and a lot to do with how you act and what you say. It is how your athletes know you and how they act when they're around you.

Your personality can have a major influence on the team's success and temperament. The dictator's philosophy is straightforward: "It's my way or the highway." In such a setting, the head coach makes all the decisions. The athlete's duty is to follow through immediately on the head coach's demands. Some serious faults exist in this approach. The athlete may perform only for the praise of the coach or to avoid his anger. Although this is a very low-level way to motivate athletes, many coaches feel more comfortable with this role because they like being in control.

The diplomat coach, on the other hand, consults his athletes about rules and penalties. In this scenario, the team establishes the conditions and consequences for group and individual behavior. You won't lose control or credibility by seeking their input; in fact, your athletes will be more motivated to follow you when you work with them in the formation of the rules that govern the team.

Diplomatic coaches involve the athletes at the first team meeting or at the first practice in arranging the rules the team needs to follow to achieve the goals they've established. The diplomat coach sees himself as a partner with the athletes and as their teacher. Dr. Patricia Lucas, principal of Manatee High School in Bradenton, Florida, states, "I always hire a teacher who can coach rather than a coach who may or may not be a good teacher. The classroom performance must be credible first. Usually, an excellent teacher will be an excellent coach. Coaches occupy a unique position with students, often spending more time with them than their parents do. This opportunity to make a positive contribution to a young person's life is a serious responsibility."

#79: Be Creative

Coaches must create motivation in much the same way an author composes an award-winning book or an artist paints on a canvas. The coach's best skills, insights, and efforts are required if effective motivation is the goal. Coaches need to give both creative and practical reflection on how they want to motivate their athletes to bring forth something within them that they didn't know they had. This requires careful planning and creative strategies. Motivation to succeed is the most important thing an athlete can have and probably the hardest thing a coach can teach. Whatever strategies you eventually employ, be sure to maintain your own identity and style when inspiring athletes.

Coaches across the country continually try to gain an edge on the competition by building better facilities, purchasing state-of-the-art equipment, and adding more personnel to their coaching staffs. All this can certainly make most teams more competitive, but coaches should consider novel ways to motivate as much as they do the purchase of a blocking sled or a new wrestling mat.

Some coaches get creative with their schedule and travel across the country to compete and socialize with other schools in distant states. Other coaches try new ways to train or new videos to show their teams. Some use the off-season for attending team-building camps or special events. You may choose to get creative with practice, with team introductions, or with p.a. announcements. Brainstorm the possibilities with your entire coaching staff and surprise your athletes.

The head coach, in short, leads by example. Your commitment, creativity, motivation, and effort establish the model assistant coaches and athletes should follow. This is an awesome task. A varsity athlete at University (HI) High School sums it up well: "An effective coach is someone who knows the game and the competition like the back of his hand. He has to be able to devote his time into coaching and making the team better both in-season an off-season. He has to push athletes to strive to be better and never give up."

4

Midseason

Jonathan Daniel/Allsport

#80: Invite Alumni

Former players, if given enough notice, often love to return to the school and teach younger athletes the techniques and tactics that helped them become successful. Their participation as instructors can enhance practices and motivate your current players to master especially difficult techniques and skills.

Along with teaching techniques, alumni can speak to the current athletes at practices or even the day before a competition. Their personal anecdotes, recollections, and advice can be especially motivating because current players will be hearing insights about competition from someone speaking from their perspectives (i.e., they can truly relate to each other). You'd be wise, however, to caution alumni not to use profanity or to denigrate an opponent. Instead, ask them to comment on honoring traditions, working hard, and achieving success.

Alumni are crucial to your program. They are the salesmen for it in your absence, and they can make strong impressions on younger athletes. Their presence is truly invaluable. Former sports broadcaster Chris Schenkel states, "If you can turn one athlete into a little kid's hero, you might keep the kid from doing something he shouldn't do later."

#81: Invite Teachers

Positive and productive relationships with teachers can have a tremendous impact on an athlete's motivation. Successful public relations for any athletic program begins in the school itself. Gaining the support of the faculty should be given the highest priority. In short, involve them by inviting them to contribute to your program.

To turn teachers into advocates of your program, try the following 12 tips:

- Talk to them about the athletes and keep them informed about the team's progress. If they are anti-athletics, address the situation. Gain support by monitoring the athletes' academic standing in their classes and assisting them with their assignments.

- Invite the teachers to attend competitions. Offer them free passes, if necessary, and thank them afterward for attending. You might even invite popular teachers to speak to the athletes before a practice or game.

- Convince them of their importance to your program. Here, you can initiate an "Adopt-an-Athlete" program in which a faculty member can become the personal "cheerleader" for an athlete on the team by writing him notes, wishing him luck, and inquiring about the games.

- Seek their advice when you confront a problem with an athlete who has previously expressed respect for that teacher. You might even request that this faculty member join a conference you might have with that athlete.

- Give each faculty member a free media guide and send each one a copy of your newsletter.

- Invite the physical education teacher to put the team through an aerobic workout at the beginning of a practice early in the week.

- Have the home economics teacher or school dietitian design a nutritional menu for athletes.

- Have teachers complete an academic progress report each week for athletes who might have grade or eligibility problems in their classes.

- Ask the advisor to the school newspaper to have student reporters write articles about selected athletes.

- Give each teacher a copy of your schedule and goals at the beginning of the season and ask that they spend a moment between classes to encourage any athlete to achieve success in his games and in accomplishing his goals.

- Ask teachers to post a copy of the schedule in their classrooms and remind all students about upcoming competitions.

- Give all teachers a list of your award winners at the end of the season so that they can congratulate them.

#82: Invite Other Coaches

You don't have to motivate your athletes alone. Your coaching colleagues would probably be honored to speak to your players and encourage them before competitions. Keep in mind that your athletes may also compete on their teams. Before you ask any other coach to speak, discuss this with your coaching staff and plan accordingly (i.e., who, when, where, and what). The "what" refers to the topic; some possibilities include goal-setting, working hard, and overcoming failure (persistence).

You can even invite opposing coaches to talk to your players, typically directly after a competition, about the progress they're making or the effort they exhibited. At least be sure to tell your athletes about the praise the team receives from opposing coaches. Most athletes are inspired when they hear they have made a positive impression on adult coaches outside their own program. Again, you should arrange this ahead of time and thank the other coach officially in a follow-up letter.

#83: Invite Local Celebrities

Asking a local celebrity to speak to the team can both bring media attention to your program and motivate athletes. A local celebrity could be an actor, performer, politician, or professional athlete, among others. In short, a celebrity is anyone who has achieved some level of fame or media attention. You may invite a local television newscaster, a former football All-American, the mayor, or a college president who lives nearby. You will find that most local celebrities enjoy speaking to athletes about setting goals, keeping a positive attitude, and being successful.

Be cautious and selective about using professional athletes to help motivate your players. Their reasons for competing (money, fame) can certainly differ from your those of your athletes, so be sure to ask only the most appropriate professionals to speak to your team. It is very important to hear the content of their talk ahead of time; don't allow them to speak off the cuff. The right pro athlete, however, can have an enormous impact on the players and truly motivate them to pursue success.

#84: Change the Routine

Don't be afraid to change the warm-up, the practice routine, or the format and intensity of each practice to prevent boredom or burnout. The major objective of each practice is simply to take each player from his present skill level to a more advanced level. If you and your staff feel that changing any part of the practice routine will increase the probability that the players can master necessary skills, then do it. These skills shouldn't be too large or complex (they should be easy to understand and perform), and of course, the coaches should provide constant reinforcement or rewards after each attempt.

Through the course of the practice, the coach should be cautious about fatigue. Indeed, as athletes' level of exhaustion increases, their level of motivation decreases. Heavy training sessions shouldn't be coupled with learning new skills. "An effective coach," says Larry Hoon, who has been a head wrestling coach for more than 32 years, "runs an organized and efficient practice and simply has a plan for success. I'm also not afraid to venture beyond the teaching of moves or techniques and spend time getting to be friends with my kids."

You should avoid introducing new techniques late in the week or late in the season because this could prompt anxiety in some athletes who then could be too absorbed with their anxiety to learn what you're trying to teach. In addition, practice should be a time for athletes to practice mental skills as well as physical ones. Their physical effort may require a lot of sweat; their mental effort requires constant concentration. Coaches should circulate around the practice area and work with all athletes—freshmen, junior varsity, and varsity. This enables each athlete to receive a lot of feedback on his skills and, therefore, make greater improvements.

In summary, adhere to the following important techniques to make practice an enjoyable and rewarding experience for your players:

- Keep them busy
- Reward dutiful attendance
- Vary the practice schedule
- Surprise them occasionally
- Allow them to give input about the practice schedule or have the more skilled athletes teach techniques to the less skilled athletes
- Allow for individual instruction on a daily basis
- Shorten practices, especially in the season's final weeks
- Have coaches circulate around the practice area and dialogue with all of the athletes

#85: Designate a Winning Time

Developing different ways to motivate a team is certainly an ongoing challenge. Each season may require new methods, but the experienced coach realizes this. A new season often means you have a new team to teach how to be successful. Consider allowing them to *teach themselves*.

Allow athletes time during practice each day to do what they want to do to make themselves better competitors. Giving them free time to make themselves better athletes is a unique motivator, one few coaches may feel comfortable employing. The process is to give athletes a 10 to 15 minute time span either at the middle or near the end of each practice to work on mastering their weakest skills—a period when they can work together or alone on the techniques or skills they need to master. In short, they're creating the foundation for their own success. Typically, you'll notice groups of three or four choosing an activity (e.g., running laps or hitting the blocking sled) and then motivating each other until the task is completed. It is not uncommon to observe seniors teaching freshmen or the talented kids encouraging the less talented.

The only rule is that all athletes must stay active (e.g., running, drilling, jumping rope, lifting) during this session. This time is allotted for them to work on skills, not rest. The coaches can also give individual attention to some athletes during this short period. When athletes are self-directed—under your observation—you can provide more individualized instruction and correct their mistakes. This also can enable them to take some element of control over their own skill development and improvement as an athlete.

Clearly, what happens for athletes at practice has a major influence on what happens for them in competitions. Make your players recognize the importance of practicing with intensity and diligence, especially when they can choose the activity. Kids have to be directed to take responsibility for their own success in practice, and when you let them do so you increase their motivation.

#86: Play Games

Don't misunderstand this idea. You still need to design practices that begin with clear objectives and involve specific activities, but inserting a game (relay races for soccer players or knee football on the mat for wrestlers) can give a tremendous psychological boost to your athletes. One baseball coach even had an Easter egg hunt out on the diamond that had players running around and scooping plastic egg shells with candy inside. The athletes were still active, but the rigor of practice was replaced, at least for a short period, by a fun activity. Once you play a game in practice you will probably hear your players request that you do it again. Use that request as a motivator (e.g.,, if everyone accomplishes a certain task in a set time limit, you can let them play a game: your players will work their hardest for the opportunity to play that game.

#87: Allow a Day Off

Don't be afraid to give a day off. You have to be flexible. On some days you may discover that your team is troubled or concerned about some school or social issue. It's interfering with their concentration on the tasks you've planned for practice, and they're sluggish through every drill. Be ready, therefore, to talk about it and make adjustments. If team members still appear troubled or upset, release this psychological burden by sharing it with them. Counter any negative feelings by giving them reasons to be excited about the upcoming competition and reviewing team—and possibly individual—goals. More importantly, don't add to their anxiety; instead, have an open forum discussion about it or release them from practice altogether. They will probably return the next day more motivated for practice and more convinced you are a coach who truly cares about their welfare.

#88: Travel in Style

Most coaches and athletes are used to the long yellow school bus or the cramped, dingy van. The bench seats can be uncomfortable on long trips and the exhaust smell sickening. Why not, instead, travel in style and surprise (and motivate) your team by traveling to a major competition in limousines or a chartered bus?

Certainly, a cost is involved. Employ a special fund raiser or ask the Booster Club to help defray that cost. Once community members recognize the importance of the competition, they may be encouraged to donate to the athletic department to enable the team to travel in style. Your players will appreciate the special attention given to them and, in turn, be motivated to perform in style as well.

#89: Involve Local Politicians

A fact of life is most politicians only gain office through elections, and a major way for them to communicate to the voting public is through the schools. Therefore, asking local politicians to support and praise the team in public is a win-win situation for both parties. Moreover, your athletes can be both impressed and motivated when the mayor or a congressperson encourages them directly and personally in a speech or by letter at any point in their season. The city council could also compose official proclamations that commend the team or any individual member. Such formal documents may involve the term "whereas" repeatedly, but most kids will get the point: the members of local government are impressed with their performances and want to acknowledge their importance to the community.

#90: Phone/E-mail Your Athletes

Cell phones and e-mail have transformed communication and wise coaches should take advantage of them to motivate their athletes. You can phone and e-mail athletes to praise, thank, or acknowledge them for their performances in practice or games. Use the telephone or e-mail to share a loss, compliment effort in practice, or to praise a performance (e.g., "I like your intensity in practice. That kind of effort will help you win this weekend." Or, "Your times are getting quicker. That's why you've won the last four meets."). Be sure that your statements are always affirmative and brief. You can talk at length if time permits and there's much to say, but avoid taking up too much of the athlete's personal time away from school. Besides, most often a succinct but significant message is more motivating than a longer one.

#91: Visit Athletes at Their Homes

By going to the homes of athletes and their families you demonstrate a commitment to their lives beyond the field, court, or mat. "It's important that the coach is more than a coach," says a middle school wrestler. "He has to understand me."

Robert Kanaby, executive director of the National Federation of State High School Associations, tells coaches: "You just don't walk away when the game is won or lost. There's a responsibility that carries itself into the locker room, into the school bus, and right on down the line."

Therefore, you should not be hesitant about visiting and talking to your players at their homes. In fact, you should maintain regular dialogues with players in situations other than practice that don't include school work or the sport. Such a visit can both strengthen your rapport with the player and his family and affirm his motivation.

#92: Send Cards and Letters

Writing a personal note to an athlete can be time-consuming, but it is another effective method for motivating athletes. Such notes can include praise for a past performance, appreciation for hard work, and/or acknowledgment of a special contribution made to the program. Avoid dealing with comments on skills or techniques; focus on praise and compliments.

These correspondences can be inspirational messages, birthday cards, advice letters, congratulatory letters, or an invitation to join the program (Figures 92-1 and 92-2). Be personal, but not pushy, and be sure to check later that the athlete did receive it.

Dear John:

Watching you on the football field this fall convinced me you have the skills and stamina to be a successful wrestler. I would bet that your hard-hitting style of play at linebacker is a key reason our team's defense is so highly ranked in the conference. I think your abilities can only get better if you compete on the wrestling team this season

Sure, it might be tough at first, but if you're not afraid of challenges and like one-on-one competition in which you don't have to depend on an entire team to make the "big play," then wrestling is the sport for you. Talk to some of the guys who are on the team and ask them about it. I'm certain they'd like to see you join.

I want to see you on the mats this winter, but for now keep up the good work on the football field. Good luck in your game against _____ High School. Be a leader!

Sincerely,

Figure 92-1. Personal note to a prospective team member

Dear _____ :

I'm glad you're reading this, and I'm betting you're eager to have a great season next year. It's time now to begin getting ready.

Ready for what?

Success. Your success. And team success.

You really showed improvement this year, and the coaches often talked about your hustle and enthusiasm. You made the most of your talent and abilities, and we are eager to see even more improvement next year. We have a lot of confidence in you.

Whatever you lack in experience can be made up with lots of desire, extra work, and perseverance. Confidence comes with preparation. So let's start preparing.

Preparing for success!

Your coach,

Figure 92-2. Personal note to a current team member

#93: Host a "Parents' Night" Contest

A "Parents' Night" event is typically near the middle or end of the season, and players are introduced along with their parents. Prior to a competition, each player escorts his parents into the gym as the announcer introduces them. An added highlight would be for each athlete to present his mother with a single flower and his father with a T-shirt that matches the school's colors. This traditional and important event can be used to motivate both the players and their parents.

#94: Host a Tournament

Encourage your administration to host one tournament—either at the junior high or high school level—to expose the student body to the excitement of the sport and the players to the excitement of individual awards. A tournament can also be advantageous to the Booster Club, which can use a weekend tournament to obtain revenues by selling food, beverages, and candy at a concession stand.

In Ohio, for example, tournaments are in operation almost every weekend of the school year—fall, winter, and spring. Competing for trophies, plaques, medals, or ribbons appeals to many athletes' extrinsic motivation, and placing in a tournament can provide the opportunity for them to receive such awards.

You may decide to attend another school's tournament instead. If that is the case, you should allow the athletes and their parents to decide the tournament(s) where they wish to compete. Be ready to provide forms, directions, and information about these tournaments to school personnel, fans, and parents.

Encourage athletes to participate in postseason tournaments as well—sports like wrestling, track, golf, tennis, basketball, and travel baseball and softball make this possible in the summer in many states. These events, scheduled annually and usually open to athletes of all ages, enable athletes to compete in the off-season at the local, state, regional, and national level and to improve their skills. The experience can do much to enhance their self-confidence for the next season and maintain the high level of motivation they have for your sport.

#95: Use Audiotapes

Since so many athletes these days have headphones and CD players, tapes and CDs from motivational speakers offers another way to motivate them. Consider purchasing or borrowing from the library the tapes or CDs produced by such noted speakers as Anthony Robbins ("Personal Power"), Jeff Keller, or Zig Ziglar and then distributing them one at a time to your athletes. You may even distribute them to players as they travel with you on a long bus ride or as they sit in the bleachers at a tournament. Be selective and preview the tapes yourself first so you know the message is one you want your players to hear. Many motivational speeches are also available for download from the Internet (e.g., www.audiomotivation.com). These files can then be loaded into a portable mp3 player and shared with your athletes.

#96: Use Books

English teachers will certainly support you with this initiative. When you prompt athletes to read books that deal with positive thinking and motivation, you not only use an effective motivational tool but also improve their reading skills. These books could be biographies of people who became successful due to their own perseverance and effort, nonfiction books about motivation and success, or even novels that deal with sports or teams. Get the books yourself and distribute them one at a time to your athletes. Or, simply provide a list of titles and request that they go to the library on their own. You might, in fact, suggest they read some of the following:

- *Great Book of Inspiring Quotations*, by Peter Klavora
- *Another 1001 Motivational Messages and Quotes*, by Bruce Brown
- *The Edge*, by Howard Ferguson
- *Purpose Lies Within: A Motivational Book for the Heart and Soul*, by Kimberly Phillips, et al.
- *Great Motivation Secrets of Great Leaders*, by John Baldoni
- *Motivation and Goal Setting*, by Jim Cairo
- *Chicken Soup for the Teenage Soul*, by Jack Canfield

Of course, many more titles are available and a search through your library catalog, a bookstore, or online can identify them for you. You might even check out several to read yourself (e.g., *The Big Book of Motivation Games*, by Robert Epstein) and come up with more ways to motivate your players.

Some athletes may read only part of the book before returning it to you, but even a single story or quote from the book could make an impact. Reading is a private experience and gives you another way to motivate athletes away from the practice area and away from their teammates. Your more introverted players may appreciate this. Plus, this type of motivation will appeal to fellow teachers, administrators, and parents.

#97: Help Seniors

A goal for many high school athletes is to receive an athletic scholarship to attend college. This is a primary motivation for them. Unfortunately, not enough college scholarships are available for all deserving high school senior athletes, even the champions. However, taking certain steps can assist any talented senior get the attention of a college coach and sustain his motivation to pursue an athletic scholarship. A letter of recommendation (Figure 97-1) and a resume (Figure 97-2) should be mailed at the midpoint of the season. This enables the college coach to monitor the athlete for the remainder of the season. Make sure a copy of both is given to the athlete and his parents.

Follow up with a brief letter or phone call at the end of the season to learn if the college coach is indeed interested in the senior athlete. Keep a file of letters written by college coaches who express an interest in any senior athletes.

Jim Vreeland, a coach and official for more than 33 years at three different Ohio high schools, realizes that coaching doesn't end when the athlete graduates. "My success as a coach," Vreeland says, "is not truly recognized until my athletes are years out of high school. My job is use athletics to help build stronger, better people who are ready to take their place in the world. My job is to make a change in the life of a young person. And there's a personal satisfaction to it, especially in helping seniors get in college and succeed at that level, too."

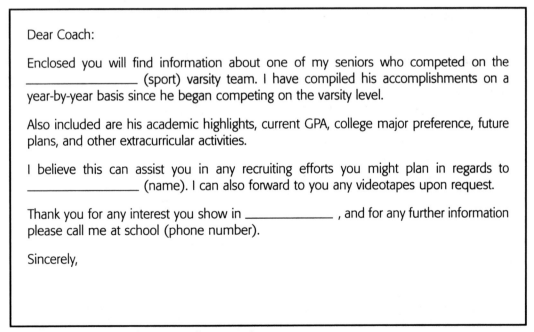

Dear Coach:

Enclosed you will find information about one of my seniors who competed on the _____ (sport) varsity team. I have compiled his accomplishments on a year-by-year basis since he began competing on the varsity level.

Also included are his academic highlights, current GPA, college major preference, future plans, and other extracurricular activities.

I believe this can assist you in any recruiting efforts you might plan in regards to _____ (name). I can also forward to you any videotapes upon request.

Thank you for any interest you show in _____ , and for any further information please call me at school (phone number).

Sincerely,

Figure 97-1. Recruiting letter to college coaches

Resume for (Name)
His Address and Phone Number

2001-2002 (Freshmen Year) Earned Varsity Letter

2nd in Conference Tournament   16-4 Record at 2nd Singles
District Qualifier   Achieved Academic Honor Roll

2002-2003 (Sophomore Year) Earned Varsity Letter

2nd at Richmond Invitational   Led the Team in Aces
2nd at Sectional Tournament   Most Improved Player Award
1st in Conference Tournament   Achieved Academic Honor Roll
District Semifinalist   Scholar Athlete Award
18-5 Record at 1st Singles

2003-2004 (Junior Year) Earned Varsity Letter

3rd in Division II State Tournament   25-2 Record at 1st Singles
District Champion   Led the Team in Aces
Sectional Champion   Inducted into National Honor Society
Conference Champion   Junior Class Vice-President
Richmond Invitational Champion   Scholar-Athlete Award Winner
News Herald Player of the Week   Varsity Letter Winner in Soccer
Team Captain   News Herald Player of the Year
MVP Award Winner   District Player of the Year

2004-2005 (Senior Year) Earned Varsity Letter
Note: *Achievements listed here reflect only the first half of this athlete's senior season.*

Varsity Team Captain   Senior Class President
Richmond Invitational Champion   NHS Vice-President
Lincoln Heights Champion   Scholar-Athlete Award Winner
News Herald Player of the Week   Varsity Letter Winner in Soccer
Rated #1 by State Tennis Association

Figure 97-2. Athlete's resume

#98: Go Out

Motivation is not restricted to the practice room, the field, or the gym. Though some coaches (and many administrators) may worry about supervision, don't be hesitant about taking your team out as a group. Possibilities here include dinner, a movie, a school play, another sport's game, a college game, or an arcade.

The point is to use this experience to build positive relationships with the athletes and to establish a rapport with them. You must be the catalyst for this relationship-building process. With rapport comes acceptance, and it follows then that everyone directly involved with the program can more easily and readily accept the validity and value of the team's objectives. This takes, to be sure, much time and effort (sometimes almost an entire season), but the ultimate reward is the faith (and motivation) all these individuals have in you and your program.

5

Postseason

Alex Livesey/Allsport

#99: Arrange a Beneficial Schedule

When scheduling the season, arrange competitions, especially tournaments, where players can compete at their level. That said, when scheduling competitions for the junior high and high school programs, be sure to compete against at least two schools outside your conference schedule who equal your team's skill level and at least two teams against whom you feel certain about success. This enables most athletes to be successful and to maintain their confidence (and motivation). Then schedule two superior teams to expose the players to the characteristics of winning programs: their aggressive style of play, conditioning, and fan support. To be sure, do not include more than two teams like this for either the junior high or high school schedule, since you don't want to damage the confidence of your athletes too easily.

You can also arrange, after receiving permission from your administration, a competition that requires your team to travel a significant distance and stay overnight. Athletes enjoy the special status and experience of traveling to a distant school and staying in hotel rooms or with host families for a game or tournament. This would certainly be a highlight of their season and add to their motivation.

Another key element to proper scheduling is to avoid any conflicts with your school's other programs. Set the starting times to promote attendance by parents and students. Be sure that your junior high athletes can attend your high school competitions for free and have your high school athletes attend at least one junior high competition as a group.

#100: Host an Awards Program

Another major requirement for most coaches and a final way to motivate players is an end-of-year awards program or banquet. At the beginning of the season, consult with the athletic director about your specific responsibilities here. Determine the types of awards you want to give out to your top athletes and the criteria that accompany each award (Figure 100-1).

Don't be afraid to share the wealth. In other words, use this event to honor and motivate as many different athletes as possible. It is also wise to allow the athletes to select (by private vote) the winner of at least one award. Typical awards include Most Improved Player (either from previous season to current season or from the beginning of the current season to its end), Coach's Award (given to the hardest working and most coachable athlete), Scholar-Athlete Award (for the most accomplished student, either by GPA or academic honors, on the team), and Most Outstanding Athlete.

Print this information and distribute it the parents and athletes at the beginning of the season, possibly at the "Meet the Team" program. Use this to motivate them right away.

At this awards program you might also choose to distribute T-shirts that declare any championships won by the team or trophies for athletes who were tops in certain statistical categories (e.g., Most Tackles, Most Points, Most Victories). Also, acknowledge and thank all assistant coaches (including junior high or middle school coaches), the principal, assistant principal, athletic director, and trainers. Express gratitude to the school's booster club and other support groups (mention mothers and fathers by name), your statisticians, and any other personnel. Announce any tournament winners and all-conference, all-district, or all-state selections; reward the varsity letter winners; and finally hand out your major awards.

Since parents are in attendance, use the time again to explain your expectations of the athletes in the off-season. You may want them to attend a summer camp, participate in conditioning sessions, compete in other school sports, or simply return some equipment or uniforms. Speak about their academics and their goals, the progress the team accomplished and the improvements that still need to come, the satisfaction you've had coaching and the concerns you have for the following season. You can also play a promotional videotape or hand out pictures taken of the athletes during the season by a school photographer. As in your first team meeting with the athletes, end on a positive note.

If organized effectively, this awards program can be a very motivational event for your athletes and their parents and a positive way to end the season.

Earning a Varsity Letter

To earn a varsity letter, an athlete must compete in more than one half of varsity games. Tournaments will count as two games. He must also compete in the Sectional Tournament.

A player could also receive a varsity letter if the coaching staff feels this individual was an integral part of the team and did the best he could considering his ability and year of graduation.

All players will be awarded Junior Varsity Awards if they do not earn a Varsity Award.

Awards

We will award the following trophies:

• **Most Outstanding Player**

Given to the varsity player who has the best won/loss record or best performance based on statistical review; who has the most total tournament titles and/or place finishes; who earns the most conference, district, regional, and state recognition; and who has demonstrated a high level of technical superiority throughout the season both in competitions and practices.

Determined by the vote of the coaching staff. Coaches' discretion in case of injury at postseason tournaments

• **Most Improved Player**

Given to the varsity player who shows the most development from the beginning to the end of the season; who increases his won/loss record or statistical ratings; who earns conference, district, regional, or state recognition or awards during the latter part of the season after failing to do so early in the season; and whose skill level in practices and competition makes the most improvement.

Determined by the vote of the coaching staff

Figure 100-1. Postseason awards

- **Most Outstanding Junior Varsity Player**

Given to the junior varsity player who has the best JV won/loss record and statistical achievements; who earns the most tournament titles or place finishes in JV competitions; and who possibly competed successfully in some varsity competitions but did not earn a varsity letter.

Determined by the vote of the coaching staff

- **Coaches' Award**

Given to the senior player who displays the most service to the sport; who maintains daily a positive attitude; who demonstrates leadership; who has high attendance; and who dedicates himself to improving his athletic skills.

Determined by the vote of the coaching staff

Note: This award winner cannot be either the Most Outstanding Player or Most Improved Player award winner.

- **Hustle Award**

Given to the player—either varsity or junior varsity—who displays the most intensity and commitment throughout the season; who has the most enthusiasm and spirit; and who shows the most determination to excel even though his physical abilities might hinder him.

Determined by vote of the entire team

Note: This individual cannot also be a winner of any other major awards.

Figure 100-1. Postseason awards cont.

#101: Assess

For one wrestling coach who has won 16 conference and 12 sectional championships, the postseason is a time for a detailed assessment. "I begin by looking ahead at least three years to see what the program needs," says Bill McGrain of Olmsted Falls (OH) High School. He also reviews losses and "pays attention to the details in order to prepare for difficult times next year. I enjoy wrestling and want to stay with it even in the off-season. I want to lead by example."

His assessment also includes the strengths and weaknesses of the ways his staff motivated both the middle school and high school wrestlers. McGrain wants to discover at the end of each season what worked and what didn't. This type of assessment can take be accomplished in several ways:

First, talk to your athletes—in the lunchroom, at workouts, after school, on the phone. Find out what truly motivated them and what didn't.

Another important conversation should be with the athletic director in which you can assess the season, order new uniforms, evaluate the assistant coaches, and review the needs of the entire program. Expect, of course, to hear some constructive criticism about your motivational techniques. Just as you continually seek improvement from your athletes, your athletic director should expect the same from you.

A discerning, analytical coach also reviews the elements that resulted in victory and then considers how to repeat them. Do not be satisfied with one winning season or one tournament title. Instead, brainstorm with your coaching staff on how to empower and motivate your athletes to re-master the strategies and skills that made them successful previously. Legendary football coach Don Shula cautions us that, "Success isn't final. Past performance is forgotten in every new competition. It is harder to stay on top than it is to get there."

An assessment at the end of the season should always involve the following questions. Consider each in terms of its relationship to effective motivation and respond honestly:

- Did you communicate effectively?
- Did you promote a team concept?
- Did you treat athletes fairly and consistently?
- Did you empathize with the kids' problems?
- Did you reflect daily a positive attitude?
- Did you establish a solid rapport with athletes?
- Did you show patience and understanding?

- Did you display a sense of humor?
- Did you develop school and team spirit?
- Did you show enthusiasm and a positive attitude?
- Did you strive to be successful and competitive?
- Did you successfully organize the entire program?
- Did you publicize the program?
- Did you help seniors attend college (or earn scholarships)?

About the Author

Keith Manos is an English teacher and the former wrestling coach and athletic director at Richmond Heights (OH) High School.

Manos was named Division III Ohio Wrestling Coach of the Year (1988), NE District Division III Wrestling Coach of the Year (1989), GCWCOA Division III Wrestling Coach of the Year (1989), and East Suburban Conference Wrestling Coach of the Year twice (1988 and 1989). The Greater Cleveland Wrestling Coaches and Officials Association honored him with their Award of Merit in 2002. Manos was the head coach of the United States All-Star Wrestling Team (vs. Oklahoma All-Stars) in 1989 and head coach of the Ohio All-Star Wrestling Team in 1991, and has coached multiple all-star wrestling teams and wrestling clubs in Toledo, Sandusky, and Cleveland.

During his tenure as a head coach Manos had 29 qualifiers to the state tournament, with 21 state tournament placers and three state champions, including Dan Hanson, a four-time state champion. In eight years at Richmond Heights High School, Manos's teams finished in the top 10 at the state tournament five times.

In 2000, Keith was also honored as Ohio's English Teacher of the Year by the Ohio Council of Teachers of English and Language Arts.

He lives in Willoughby, Ohio, with his wife, Cheryl, daughter, Brittny, and twin sons, John-Morgan and Christian.